The Nature of Theology

The Nature of Theology

Challenges, Frameworks, Basic Beliefs

ROGER HAIGHT, SJ

ORBIS BOOKS
Maryknoll, New York 10545

Manufactured in the United States of America.
Manuscript editing and typesetting by Joan Weber Laflamme.

Library of Congress Cataloging-in-Publication Data

Names: Haight, Roger, author.
Title: The nature of theology : challenges, frameworks, basic beliefs / Roger Haight, SJ.
Description: Maryknoll, NY : Oribis Books, [2022] | Includes bibliographical references and index. | Summary: "Describes the logic of Christian theology by sidestepping an abstract analysis of the discipline and offering a relatively clear structure of the discipline of theology that is responsive to our current situation"— Provided by publisher.
Identifiers: LCCN 2022003358 (print) | LCCN 2022003359 (ebook) | ISBN 9781626984882 (print) | ISBN 9781608339501 (ebook)
Subjects: LCSH: Theology.
Classification: LCC BR118 .H344 2022 (print) | LCC BR118 (ebook) | DDC 230—dc23/eng/20220404
LC record available at https://lccn.loc.gov/2022003358
LC ebook record available at https://lccn.loc.gov/202200335

Contents

Part Three
The Content of Christian Theology: Basic Beliefs

Introduction

Thirty years ago I published a book on the basic components of Christian theology.[1] Although this work incorporates or presupposes much of that earlier work, the many differences between them offer insight into developments over the years and what is going on in this book.

In *Dynamics of Theology* I was concerned that the discipline of theology should have greater methodological self-consciousness within the confines of a professional school of ministry. Law schools and medical schools seemed to be more rigorous in their research and critical in their interpretation. Christian theology has a long history of being a critical academic discipline, and professional schools demand no less. But critical questioning does not have to translate into inaccessible language. That book was thus written to address a larger audience than professional theologians.

Dynamics considered faith to be a common human response to reality, but distinct from the formal statements of belief that are changeable expressions of a consistent faith commitment. Revelation too had to be sharply distinguished from communication of heavenly information. As in the case of faith, Christian ministers needed nuanced reflection on how scripture could be appropriated in a culture that asks questions about everything. *Dynamics* offered a systematic account of the symbolic structure of religious and theological language and a critical hermeneutical method for appropriating the tradition. Overall, the book was addressed to insiders, Christian ministers who had to address people who were

---

[1] Roger Haight, *Dynamics of Theology* (Mahwah, NJ: Paulist Press, 1990; republished Maryknoll, NY: Orbis Books, 2001).

asking ever more sophisticated questions about the beliefs of their own churches.

Three decades have generated remarkable changes in Western intellectual culture that help account for the differences between this and that earlier work. Major political and social events on the national and world stage, not to mention behaviors mediated by technological developments, helped stimulate shifts in secular and church cultures. We can point to a few developments that help to account for significant shifts in the context of theology.

First of all, the last thirty years have witnessed a decline in church participation. Moreover, opinion polls indicate that active church members do not relate to the formal teachings of their churches in an uncritical way but are privately or publicly selective. Some have no interest at all in theological distinctions, and Christianity tends to be reduced to practice. These large social adjustments are accompanied by developments that have challenged some specific theological assumptions or beliefs. Isolating certain problems can help to frame the situation of theology today.

Four clusters of issues exercise deep influence on Christian self-understanding today. The first arises from a dialogue with science, which to many Christians appears as an enemy of theology. An implicit internalization of the disciplinary premises of some sciences, such as empiricism and materialism, subtly affects a theological imagination. The suppositions and authority of the sciences seep into consciousness and tend to weaken the status of theological claims to truth about God and God's relationship with human existence.

A second area of theological contention lies in the extensive development of liberation theologies: they have expanded consciousness to a range of oppressive behaviors. As pluralistic societies have pushed religious belonging toward a private sphere, liberation theologies have invited members of the churches toward public institutional positions on issues of the common good that not all the members are willing to embrace. This area is particularly difficult because public social rhetoric lends itself less to nuance and careful thinking and more to exaggerated impressionism. Churches have become socially polarized organizations rather than houses of reconciliation.

A third area of change has to do with public acceptance of other religious traditions as authentic and veridical. A positive appreciation of the historical contexts of religions has begun to challenge a long tradition of Christian supremacy. People of other religious traditions are listening in on Christian discussions. This gradual awakening to religious pluralism has a wide variety of implications for different Christian groups, but no one should doubt the depth of the gradual change of worldview that is affecting more and more people.

A fourth area of Christian theology under scrutiny is Christology. A Christian imagination that is more open to religious pluralism invites questions about the meaning of the divinity of Jesus Christ. The issue is deep, and its implications are fraught.

These issues were on the table thirty years ago; they have been discussed for a long time. But they have come to the fore in a more pressing, self-conscious way. These issues do not isolate theology today from its traditional forms; many traditional distinctions are still relevant. But these problems help to explain some of the perspectives and demands on theological reasoning. New creative tensions are in the air. Students of theology are less homogeneous than ever before; church-related schools are open to a larger public. Interfaith issues are more telling and engaging than ecumenical issues. The dialogue with science represents new exigencies for authority; an imagination schooled in science offers challenges to the framework and suppositions of theology. How can theology maintain a real authority in its exchange with scientific culture and a critically informed political culture? If religious pluralism means one religious tradition can learn from other religions, how does theology justify the particular claims of its tradition? If theology arises out of a faith community, how does it retain its autonomy as an academic discipline relative to the more objective disciplines of social sciences and religious studies?

These generalizations about changes in the context and form of theology materialize in the students in today's universities and graduate schools. Many young Christians are unschooled in the religion of their birth; they know some words but have little idea of their meaning. Others have been instructed in their faith, but they have appropriated it in uncritical, anthropomorphic terms; they fiercely hold to these terms against secular forms of knowledge that seem to threaten faith. Interestingly, as well, while some people are leaving the churches, others are turning toward Christian faith as seekers, some educated and some not, and they approach with no real knowledge of Christian beliefs. Suppose all of these people are part of the audience to whom one wants to introduce the discipline of Christian theology. How would one design such a course? Where would one begin? What conception of the discipline, in the sense of its basic design, will the course represent? These questions represent a practical attitude to the subject matter addressed in this discussion.

But the questions also carry deeper dimensions. Has Christian theology devolved into an intrinsically eclectic discipline? While theology as a discipline of undergraduate and graduate education naturally subdivides into multiple sub-disciplines or fields, the focus often falls on what is called systematic or constructive theology. But within that designation, courses vary considerably in method and subject matter. Courses that bear the same title sometimes do not resemble one another in either approach or content. What is it, then, that determines whether they represent the same discipline? Can one determine an internal structure of Christian theology today that makes it an integral humanistic discipline with relatively clear boundaries? This discussion seeks to go beyond transcendentalism, that is, a universal anthropological base, in search of a common structure that makes Christian theology a focused, practical, and humanistic academic discipline that can address the variety of people who study it in our time.

The quest for a practical rather than an intellectual organizational principle should not be read as an abandonment of the gains made in the last two centuries. One can recognize the integrating power of a transcendental definition of theology, for example, in the theologies of Friedrich Schleiermacher, Rudolf Bultmann, Karl Rahner, and Bernard Lonergan, as a permanent contribution to the field. The stability of the human species and of the structure of the human mind offer ways of organizing theological questions and Christian answers. Human beings can still communicate with one another across radical historical and cultural differences. Recognition of historical consciousness does not contradict transcendental thinking. But historical consciousness attends to the unique context, to the distinct situations and particular problems of our time and place. It focuses the imaginative horizon for understanding on the present and integrates into the foundations of theology a human response to problems publicly encountered. Rather than a counterproposal, simply in distinction from transcendental theology, responding more directly to present-day situations and cultures defines the practical character of theology. It directs the attention of a critical intellect to the questions that people are actually asking.[2] The diversity within theology reflects a search for a common relevant structure of the discipline in a wildly fragmented human experience. This book describes the logic of Christian theology by sidestepping an abstract analysis of the discipline and its various methodologies. It begins instead with our cultural situation and the intellectual and practical problems that face us.

The book aims at outlining a relatively clear structure of the discipline of theology that is responsive to the current situation.[3] It seeks to replace "reflection on God" and "faith seeking understanding" as its first definition. A more descriptive conception of theology sees it as interpretation of the world from the perspective of the symbols of the Christian faith tradition. Theology must begin by describing our situation in terms of cultural motifs that all recognize.

This account proposes that three major challenges to the Christian faith characterize a context that Christian theology must address.

---

[2] What is proposed here bears analogy to Dorothee Soelle's early statement (*Political Theology* [Philadelphia: Fortress Press, 1974]) in response to Rudolf Bultmann's existential theology; Johann Baptist Metz ("Transcendental-Idealistic or Narrative-Practical Christianity? Theology and Christianity's Contemporary Identity Crisis," in *Faith in History and Society: Toward a Practical Fundamental Theology* [New York: Crossroad, 2007]) in response to Karl Rahner's transcendental theology; later Edward Schillebeeckx's response to his own earlier Neo-Thomism; and James Cone in response to his formative Barthianism. These examples do not necessarily represent competitive differences but new, practical, historically conscious approaches that include the former theologies but direct them to a more pointed and specific humanistic horizon.

[3] This work reflects research done in several distinct areas of theology over decades. The point is not to introduce new theological opinion, but to open up a discussion of the distinctive character of Christian theology as an autonomous academic discipline alongside others. This is done in a constructive rather than a polemic or comparative way. It does not conclude the conversation but contributes to it.

The three problems are metaphysical skepticism, relativism, and ontic pessimism. In various ways these issues help account for the explosion of courses that pass as theology. In this book these cultural biases set formal exigencies for the discipline: responding to them gives theology a credibility it would otherwise lack, as they underlie some of the deepest human questions of our time. This move and the claim behind it depend on an axiom concerning the historical situatedness of all human understanding; namely, that the historical, social, and cultural situation constitutes an intrinsic dimension of the way anything is understood, and that it influences the content of knowing itself.

The three challenges provide the implicit logic of how the chapters unfold. Part One, which contains Chapter 1, briefly develops the three problems just mentioned that dominate the discipline and to which theology must respond in order to be credible. Part Two comprises Chapters 2, 3, and 4. They bear a formal character, meaning that they develop a framework for a holistic approach to theology by addressing each of the three problems and highlighting their significance for theology today. In other words, the contemporary form of Christian theology shows that it is aware of these problems and engages them. Finally, Part Three presents the content of Christian theology in Chapters 5, 6, and 7. They too respond to the problems that challenge Christian self-understanding with commentary on basic beliefs: God as creator; Jesus as a mediator with universal relevance; and God as Spirit. As an introduction to Christian theology rather than a systematic or constructive synthesis, these chapters on content are appropriately schematic and not extensively developed.

This threefold structure may seem overwrought. If the order of presentation seems contrived or forced, at least it serves to integrate into theology's definition newly relevant and deeply felt human problems that affect its credibility, method, and initial presentation. The issues challenging theology are both historical and metaphysical; they call into question both the possibility and the relevance of theology as a coherent academic pursuit. Ignoring them trivializes the discipline itself.

Part One

The Three Problems

1

The Challenges
of Culture

This book deals with the academic discipline of theology. As an academic discipline, theology transcends simple reflection on the subject matter of religious faith. It strives to conform to standard requirements of intellectual study. Wondering about the stars that grace the night sky does not make one an astronomer. So too, many people who belong to a discernible faith tradition learn about the content of their religion and reflect on it without becoming students of theology. The sources of Christian theology were written in the ordinary religious language of ancient cultures, and theology critically appropriates that primary language in the measured reflective language of a new culture.[1]

Theology is an ongoing and never-ending project. It moves forward in the wake of history. It always reflects the particular cultural situation of its making; it is always directed to a particular audience. This book reflects the developed world of the West, in particular North American culture. But theology is not mathematics; other works describing this academic discipline would carry different accents. This introduction to theology attends to the distinctive demands upon theology made by the temper of present time. It inquires whether other theologians experience the same pressures.

---

[1] See Paul Ricoeur, *The Symbolism of Evil* (New York: Harper & Row, 1967), 347–57.

Recent Past

Theology is a constant process of interpretation of the world in the light of the symbols at the source of a faith tradition. It consults the landmark theologians who have handed on the tradition, the community's formative theologians at any given time, and the questions that need to be answered. The practice is continuous; there are no breaks, for even radical shifts reflect a reaction against the conditions in place. We do not need a history of modern theology here, but one has to take notice of some major cultural events following the Second World War.

The term *globalization* summarizes many of the historical developments that have affected the world-consciousness of our period. The word *globalization* refers to several different aspects of our history; it bears different interpretations and valuations. It has political associations with colonialism; it elicits positive and negative economic appreciations of capitalism; it carries connotations of hegemony; and by reaction aspirations of freedom and autonomy. Whether or not the term can be value free, it objectively describes a new interconnectedness of humanity, a new speed of communication and travel, and a new kind of electronically assisted world-consciousness. Human beings now have a concrete sense of a single species of human individuals. One can no longer grow up thinking the world is Christian or Buddhist, Hindu or Muslim.

Ideas of universal value and relevance have been altered by a new sense of polycentrism. Every country shows the map of the world with itself at the center. The scientific and technological developments of the West have long been undergirded by a sense of Christian supremacy. By contrast, globalization has helped introduce a new sense of continental, national, and regional identity. There will always be strategic geopolitical thinking, but interdependence has forced a new respect for other autonomous ways of life.

The idea of *urbanization* captures another line of development since the Second World War. Not only has the size of cities grown, but the contrast between the possibilities offered by urban life as contrasted with rural agrarian or mountain culture is dramatic. The whole world became accessible in large cities: diversity, career possibilities, wealth and poverty, crime, suffering, and artistic creativity. The pluralism of the city reflects the diversity of the world, different political organizations, approaches to education, and a variety of approaches to theology.

The twentieth century experienced an abundance of human tragedy. Its hallmark in terms of numbers lies in war: killing and wounding for life. Two world wars and several attempts at genocide have been followed by a proliferation of local conflicts fed by international arms sale. The world has also gained a better understanding of the systemic character of world poverty and human discrimination. The so-called problem of evil that has always shadowed theology was often understood in terms of the innocent suffering of someone like Job. Suffering today appears much more like a pervasive social condition too often taken for granted, if not greeted with indifference.

In some ways the rational individualism of the Enlightenment and the historical consciousness of nineteenth-century academia trickled down into common consciousness in the second half of the twentieth century. University education expanded after the war, the pluralism of the cities provided freedom from small-town thinking, and critical education undermined traditions and exposed students to new ideas. The rationalism of the Enlightenment took the form of a critical social consciousness that could question everything in terms of perspective and bias. The plurality of approaches in every non-quantitative academic field communicated a sense of openness if not relativity. Everything was exposed to debate.

Enlightenment as critique was aimed at authority and especially at the churches. Immanuel Kant summed up the movement with the challenge, "Dare to think." He thus announced the autonomy of the human subject and the inviolate principle of present-day academia that each person is responsible for his or her own thought. Language about God sounds to some like alienation: it infantilizes the human person and violates the ideal of freedom as self-possession. One has to take responsibility for what one holds to be true; it must be ratified by one's own inner experience.[2] But this line of thinking seems like a mortal threat to a received confessional faith.

Finally, general education carried a bias against the anthropomorphism that underlies much of religious language. Science questions the religious ideas of God intervening into the web of natural forces; upon reflection, the stories of God seem like historicized myths, and political emancipation from religion correlates with a steady secularization of the mind. Gradually the difference between ordinary religious language and a critically educated mind developed a potential to open up students' imaginations to an ultimate void.

Postmodernity

In 1990, David Tracy wrote a penetrating essay that described the current situation for Christian theology. He pointed to the large problems facing a theologian: the consumerization of every theological vision; the problems of otherness and difference in a globalized and pluralistic world; the problem of enormous social suffering. The essay noted the breakdown of the naive anthropomorphism in much of premodern theology and the filtering of Enlightenment critique and historicist consciousness into a generally educated population in an increasingly secular culture.[3] Tracy used three large categories—modernity, anti-modernity, and postmodernity—to characterize theological responses to the situation. His typology provides background for an appreciation of the context thirty years later.

The modernity he describes grew out of Western culture. It favors a confidence in reason against authority, a turn to the instrumental reason of science, and pragmatic technological solutions to human problems. It reflects the individualism of the age, one that is competitive without compassion. But it also shows signs of a concern for

---

[2] Langdon Gilkey, *Naming the Whirlwind: The Renewal of God-Language* (Indianapolis: Bobbs-Merrill, 1969), 57–61.

[3] David Tracy, "On Naming the Present," in *On Naming the Present: God, Hermeneutics, and the Church* (Maryknoll, NY: Orbis Books, 1994), 3–24.

justice and democracy and a mystical-political or mystical-prophetic concern for social misery throughout the world. Reason supplies the universal, common, and inclusive bond that all can rely on.[4]

Those who propose alternatives to a modern outlook on the world are either anti-modern or postmodern. The anti-moderns reject the modern and seek to restore in different ways the values of the Christian vision that were prominent in a premodern situation. For example, fundamentalism resists rational critique and democratic society; it clings to Christian truths in their traditional form when they undergirded society. More critical evangelicals and the dogmatic traditions stress the word of God or church teachings as interrupting the ways of human beings, human culture, and merely human values. These voices offer serious critiques of over-confidence in human progress.

Postmoderns are mainly negative in their critiques of modernity, deconstructionists of established premises rather than builders of new systems. Postmodernity represents the death of the modern Cartesian, or Kantian, or transcendental reasoning subject. The particular, the individual, otherness, uniqueness, difference, excess, the subjugated, the excluded, and the repressed all question the normativity of universality, sameness, routine, and the established order. Reality cannot be harnessed by any particular point of view, or language, or system, or total conception of the whole.

Tracy concludes his analysis by finding within the whirlwind of conflicting frameworks strong currents of mystical-prophetic resistance and hope. But they make no headway in turbulent waters: the problems surrounding nature and ecology within a new vision of the cosmos; a theology of religions that respects each one to the point of indifference to norms and truth; and the overwhelming issues of social justice. These problems have not been resolved but have become even more pervasive. The situation for theology today can be measured by how deeply these issues affect wider consciousness within the developed world and in urban cultures beyond it.

---

[4] Sigmund Freud, *The Future of an Illusion*, trans. James Strachey (New York: W. W. Norton, 1961), 54–55.

Metaphysical Skepticism

A description of the context of theology in the developed world of North America has to be abstract enough to be comprehensive and realistic enough to represent experience. Three large categories, in some measure overlapping and redundant, may assist in the description: metaphysical skepticism, relativism, and ontic pessimism.[5] These are not objective terms; they point to dimensions of corporate consciousness that subsist at various strengths on different levels of consciousness. Objective historical developments have given rise to these filters of perception, but they do not always amount to necessary or even precise or calibrated convictions. But they are there, in persons and groups, as questions or suspicions, as doubts or opinions, that resonate in culture and within the critical theologian. One might call them problems with which theology must contend, but they really represent current manifestations of the mystery of human existence that harbors endless questions.

It remains difficult to measure on a cultural level how deeply or pervasively metaphysical skepticism affects religious consciousness. History can describe its development. But it subsists today in several convictions that are widely taken for granted: the separation of church and state; privatization of religious commitment; secularization; disenchantment; and the contrast between theology and scientific naturalism, perceived by many as a conflictive relationship.

Developed nations take for granted the separation of church and state despite the frequent disputes that manifest unclear boundaries. A comparison with the medieval wrangling between popes and kings, and the strangely similar contest between Calvin and Geneva's city magistrates in early modern Europe, show that "separation" is salutary. Institutional loyalties to church and state flow from dif-

---

[5] Analogous categories can be found in Francis Schüssler Fiorenza, "Systematic Theology: Task and Methods," *Systematic Theology: Roman Catholic Perspectives*, 2nd ed. (Minneapolis: Fortress Press, 2011), 50–54; David Tracy, *Fragments: The Existential Situation of Our Time* (Chicago: University of Chicago Press, 2020), 139.

ferent spheres of human response to reality, and each performs best when kept distinct. But the separation has consequences: religious conviction tends to become private and civic life tends to become secularized. Religious freedom is basic. Freedom of conscience before God is fundamental; religious freedom cannot be coerced by government or institutional church. That religious commitments are personal and enjoy the rights of privacy is part of the foundation of modernity. In parallel, on the public institutional level, various spheres of life, like science and bureaucratic management in a pluralist society, have to operate *etsi Deus non daretur*.[6]

Secularization names another facet of contemporary life that accompanies the separation of church and state and privatization. It describes the "process of functional differentiation and emancipation of the secular spheres—primarily the state, the economy, and science—from the religious sphere and the concomitant differentiation and specialization of religion within its own newly found religious sphere."[7] Secularization theory was generally wrong in predicting the demise of religion in modern developed societies and their disengagement from social and governmental policy. Secularization takes different forms in different societies and cultures. But secularization differentiates competencies and authority; it has left

---

[6] "As if God does not exist." José Casanova, *Public Religions in the Modern World* (Chicago: University of Chicago Press, 1994), 40. There is much more to be said about religious privatization, and Casanova's work is measured: "The central thesis of the present study is that we are witnessing the 'deprivatization' of religion in the modern world. By deprivatization I mean the fact that religious traditions throughout the world are refusing to accept the marginal and privatized role which theories of modernity as well as theories of secularization had reserved for them. Social movements have appeared which either are religious in nature or are challenging in the name of religion the legitimacy and autonomy of the primary secular spheres, the state and the market economy. Similarly, religious institutions and organizations refuse to restrict themselves to the pastoral care of individual souls and continue to raise questions about the inter-connections of private and public morality and to challenge the claims of the subsystems, particular states and markets to be exempt from extraneous normative considerations" (ibid., 5).

[7] Ibid., 19.

undisturbed whole swaths of life that are autonomous and frequently hostile to any appeal to religious authority.[8]

Secularization as a social process meets religion at several inter-sections, but the one that has a deep impact on theology is found in the imagination. Imagination here refers to the inner ability of the human mind to construct or project in front of itself an understand-ing or a goal. The logic of science is projection and verification; it imagines, and it verifies. The idea of the secular summons many associations; it remains a complex term. But within its various meanings subsists a pragmatic demand for what David Tracy has called the "disenchantment with mystifications."[9] Theology must be comprehensible in relation to present-day reality. The faith of secularity itself consists of "that fundamental attitude which affirms the ultimate significance and final worth of our lives, our thoughts, and actions, here and now, in nature and in history."[10]

Science is one of the areas freed from religious tutelage. The dialogue between theology and science had been going on construc-tively during the whole course of the development of Christianity in the West. But after Darwin's *The Origin of Species*, science became too mathematical and technical for the general public to absorb. A constructive dialogue between theologians and scientists continues, but by committee, because few can be expert in both areas. Moreover, clear boundaries methodologically distinguish a scientific and a theological imagination and ensure the autonomy of each area of knowledge. But the ability to make this distinction requires a sophistication that is not readily available in the culture at large. Metaphysical skepticism begins there but runs more deeply.

It is difficult to describe metaphysical skepticism convincingly because it contains several variables. Metaphysics as used here refers to an abstract, constructed conception of the basic structures of real-ity, how they are perceived, and the way they function. Some have

---

[8] For example, religions have lost their authority in the worlds of science, international business and trade, the politics of pluralistic democratic societies, law, medicine, and the university classroom.

[9] David Tracy, *Blessed Rage for Order: The New Pluralism in Theology* (New York: Seabury Press, 1975), 4.

[10] Ibid., 8.

argued for the demise of metaphysics; others maintain that consistent behavior patterns of human beings imply an internal metaphysical map. Metaphysics as a constructive enterprise comes close to the basic beliefs of a religious faith commitment. The sheer diversity of lifestyles and worldviews surely encourages metaphysical skepticism. For many, the autonomy, success, and authority of science and its divorce from religion seals the conviction. But such a generalized conviction itself begins to look like a metaphysical stance.

Scientism refers either to an epistemological position or an attitudinal conviction that "only science can tell us what exists, and that only science can effectively address our moral and existential questions."[11] It essentially holds that only what science can account for counts as knowledge of the really real. Other forms of knowledge represent a derivative kind of perception of reality. The main problems with scientism congeal in the many other forms of knowing that seem to represent certain truth. By contrast, the claims to truth that support scientism occupy a narrow range of empirically based conceptions. In other words, the empirical basis of science has allowed it to teach us much about the world and ourselves, but in the end, it communicates a limited kind of knowledge. Still, scientistic bias exists. It undermines, at least on the level of naive realism, the validity of anthropomorphic religious consciousness, that is, the ordinary language of popular religion, and tends toward metaphysical skepticism.[12]

For example, Sean Carroll lays out a physicist's "core theory" of reality, a description of the structure of an atom with the forces that hold subatomic particles together, the all-pervasive forces of gravity and electromagnetism, and the fields that provide the ground out of which atoms arise. Such is the given; there is nothing behind or beneath or above it. "There may be no ultimate answer to the 'Why?' question. The universe simply is, in this particular way, and

---

[11] Jeroen de Ridder, Rik Peels, and René van Woudenberg, *Scientism: Prospects and Problems* (New York: Oxford University Press, 2018), 1.

[12] Mikael Stenmark, *Scientism: Science, Ethics, and Religion* (London: Routledge, 2016), 91–103. More needs to be said here about the role of primary religious language, how it functions, its deeper symbolic structure, and the role of theology in relation to it as critically supportive rather than destructive.

that's a brute fact. Once we figure out how the universe behaves at its most comprehensive level, there will not be any deeper layers left to discover."[13] This leads toward metaphysical skepticism; there is no ultimate, objective, scientific moral grounding. "But that's how the world is. We should recognize that our desire for an objective grounding for morality creates a cognitive bias, and should compensate by being especially skeptical of any claims in that direction."[14]

Today's culture has been influenced by the sciences. Goaded by pluralism, the ethics of scientific understanding demands evidence. Science and technology enjoy great prestige across cultures because they are grounded in physical evidence. It is not enough to reassert the tradition or received opinion. An intellectual proposal must rest on evidence. The rate of social and cultural development enhances this necessity. One cannot claim a worldview "is believable because the tradition has believed it."[15] Science works. People across the world have been impressed by the way science, with a vaccine, can save so many from the fear of imminent death during a pandemic. Science gains its success and its authority precisely by limiting its sphere of knowledge to the empirical and measurable. The restriction of its ken determines the massive success of its methods not only for human living but also for social bonding: science transcends cultural divisions even when it is not recognized.

Humanists rightly complain of instrumental reason and reductionism when one leaves aside other forms of knowing. But the obvious character of this charge does not meet the challenge of science to the discipline of theology. Theology cannot go around science. It

---

[13] Sean Carroll, *The Big Picture: On the Origins of Life, Meaning, and the Universe Itself* (New York: Dutton, 2016), 203.

[14] Ibid., 402. Note that Carroll is not a moral relativist but a moral constructivist. Each culture constructs its moral norms; he denies a universal metaphysical basis for morality. "We are floating in a purposeless cosmos, confronting the inevitability of death, wondering what any of it means. But we're only adrift if we choose to be. Humanity is graduating into adulthood, leaving behind the comfortable protocols of its childhood upbringing and being forced to fend for itself. It's intimidating and wearying, but the victories are all the more sweet" (ibid., 431–32).

[15] Tracy, *Blessed Rage for Order*, 6.

has to recognize the pragmatic realism of science and chasten its own extrapolations lest they seem to be projection. Theology cannot credibly rest with a transcendence above the empirical but must find God within it. Science and theology represent two different forms of consciousness, but they can both be entertained by a single person. It is the relation between them that requires clarification. This may be a considerable test for theology, which tends to fall back on its autonomous sources and drift away from empirical life.

Relativism

For over fifty years theology has been constructively engaged in addressing the historical reality that there are many different religions. Many Christians have come to expect, to welcome, and to learn from the differences among them.[16] But development has become deeply problematic for those religions that take an absolutist or supremacist position that theirs is the only true or highest form of faith. A straightforward discussion on this problem requires some basic distinctions from the sociology of knowledge. The term *plurality* refers to sheer multiplicity and difference, as in a plurality of living species. *Pluralism* means something subtler: difference within a wider unity. As Peter Berger notes, "Pluralism is a social situation in which people with different ethnicities, worldviews, and moralities live together peacefully and interact with each other amicably."[17] The unity here is a common sphere of reference within

---

[16] This oversimplifies things; the United States offers mixed data. Authors like Robert Putnam, David E. Campbell, Robert Wuthnow, Diana Eck, Nicholas Rescher, and William Connolly celebrate American openness to pluralism. But conservative Christianity lives on, and society is still marked by racism and ethnic intolerance.

[17] Peter L. Berger, *The Many Altars of Modernity: Toward a Paradigm for Religion in a Pluralist Age* (Boston: De Gruyter, 2014), 1. Stressing the intentional character of pluralism, Pamela E. Klassen and Courtney Bender define pluralism as "a commitment to recognize and understand others across perceived or claimed lines of religious difference" (*After Pluralism: Reimagining Religious Engagement* [New York: Columbia University Press, 2010], 1).

which the different views are encountered and freely allowed to coexist and interact. Organizational examples are provincial governments within a federal government, or the churches in the World Council of Churches. With pluralism people recognize the differences and engage one another across the boundaries.

Relativism runs deeper and undermines foundations. It means that, on the level of universally relevant and objective knowledge, plurality cancels the possibility of normative truth. Metaphysical principles and seemingly universal values so relate to particular historical conditions that truth in transcendent matters does not exist or cannot be found. All candidates for objective moral or religious standards are merely functional; they are tainted by identity, class, power, or other perspectival interest. Relativism is always negative relative to universal truth; it leaves humanity with no stable, all-encompassing, or unifying values at all.[18]

These epistemological and in effect metaphysical theories affect theology in two distinct ways. One is that plurality or the sheer diversity of religious consciousness, even when softened by ideas of pluralism, easily slides into an implicit relativistic consciousness. Some discussions of pluralism scarcely distinguish it from relativism. "Pluralism relativizes and thereby undermines many of the certainties by which human beings used to live. Put differently, certainty becomes a scarce commodity."[19] The structure of religious consciousness bears metaphysical weight. Theology needs an epistemology of the sources of faith and revelation that ground its truth while recognizing its status as one among many. The other seeks a positive conception of the grounds of religious faith that accommodates pluralism. It has to explain how pluralism itself can be understood as consistent with what the long history of Christian supremacy stood for in the past even though it is no longer credible.

The first issue requires a distinctive theological analysis of the dynamics of faith and the character of revelation. But these

---

[18] "Relativism can be simply defined as the embrace of relativity; that is, the relativization that has in fact occurred is celebrated as a superior form of knowledge. One cannot be certain about anything because there is no absolute cognitive or normative truth" (Berger, *The Many Altars of Modernity*, 11).

[19] Ibid., 9.

constructions must be set in the larger horizon of the sociology of knowledge, which deals less with truth and error and more directly with the social conditioning of all knowing. The analysis prescinds from the question of truth to consider the social influence on the knowing process itself. It "does not signify that there are no criteria of rightness and wrongness in a discussion. It does insist, however, that it lies in the nature of certain assertions that they cannot be formulated absolutely, but only in terms of the perspective of a given situation."[20]

The sociology of knowledge breaks open a tacit individualist perspective on knowledge, philosophy, and religion, and it operates on the premise that history and society function as intrinsic conditions of the knowing process. Recognition of the transcendent character of the object of religious faith alters the naivety that allows religious beliefs to command a comprehensive grasp of ultimate reality. Insight into the intrinsic social conditioning of religious faith further attenuates its absolute character and opens it up to dialogue. A carefully critical appreciation of the social construction of religious beliefs can change the character of the interchange between religions from competition to conversation. Because all knowledge is situational or culturally influenced, historical consciousness calls for comparison, contrast, and mutual exchange. The engagement of religious convictions in dialogue is not a zero-sum game; communicating is not competitive. One learns from others, always looking for a higher or broader perspective, a new framework, in which to express the particular truths of one's tradition.[21]

But this position seems to be far too irenic and conceals what Kierkegaard called the inner passion of religious faith. On the one hand, existentially, the description of relationism, as Mannheim described his position, seems to compromise what comes down to

---

[20] Karl Mannheim, *Ideology and Utopia: An Introduction to the Sociology of Knowledge* (1936) (New York: Harcourt Brace, 1985), 283. Mannheim's early work in the sociology of knowledge gives it a directness and clarity that make subtle distinctions accessible. Another early and reliable text is Peter L. Berger, *The Social Construction of Reality: A Treatise in the Sociology of Knowledge* (Garden City, NY: Doubleday, 1967).

[21] Mannheim, *Ideology and Utopia*, 300–302.

"absolute" commitments. Value response ought to correspond with the value to which it clings; if God is absolute creator, an absolute commitment to God is appropriate. An experience of God or an ultimate transcendent reality within religious mediations will not easily yield to an egalitarian pluralism of mediators without some ranking. On the other hand, the very character of ultimate reality exceeds our predications by its absolute transcendence. The differences of perception among the many faith traditions demonstrates that beliefs are historically conditioned. Plurality actually testifies to the transcendent character of ultimate reality, the perspectival character of all faith, and the partial character of all religious truth. Plurality invites pluralism as the framework for comparative theology.

But this raises still another issue. How does pluralism fit with traditional Christian claims? The invitation of pluralism poses a problem not only for Christianity, but for all faith traditions that consider themselves as the highest or the only true religion. Traditionalists of any religious tradition will be sensitive to relativism, and present-day openness to pluralism will insist on respect for other religious traditions on their own terms. Theology attuned to culture today cannot escape this dilemma.

Ontic Pessimism

The term *ontic* does not carry a technical meaning. It refers to an existential consciousness that forms part of the intrinsic "ontological" condition of a person's being. The pessimism ranges from a sense of finitude and existential anxiety in the face of life's negativities to a perception, perhaps overwhelmed by suffering and pain, that life is really not worth living. Rather than beginning with a precise reconstruction of such pessimism, the discussion describes how it relates to a Christian religious consciousness.

What is called the problem of evil challenges faith's commitment to the all-powerful creator God and the conviction that God is good and loves creation. We cannot understand how God could be both good and omnipotent while having created the world as it is. The evil and suffering we witness in the world call either God's goodness or God's omnipotence into question. Whether or not the problem is exactly so formulated, a common verdict arrived at by many people holds "that the enormous amounts of seemingly pointless evils give us sufficient evidence to think that, probably, there is no God."[22]

The meaning of evil and how it relates to a religious conscious-ness have to take into account the various ways in which people encounter evil. Evil comes in many forms, and people participate in or experience it in as many different ways as there are human beings. Some persons live lives that are relatively free of the kind of pain and suffering that make up the common lot of the destitute poor who are always hungry. Some deprived people are blessed with relatively good health in contrast to an affluent person with a lifelong sickness. If we think of evil as a collection of forces, situations, or events that attack the integrity of sentient but especially human beings, conscious participation in evil varies enormously.

Marilyn McCord Adams considers "horrendous evils."[23] This refers to existential suffering of such a degree that the very worth of one's life seems to be forfeited. The deep and inescapable struc-ture of these evils defeats every reason for being. These evils are objective and real, but they involve human participation. Ordinarily participation is passive: people are affected by evil. We may not think of natural disasters as evils, but we cannot think of cancer as something good. People ask whether there is a reason for nature turning against human life. Predatory behavior is not evil in nature, but is so among humans. Moral evil involves active human partici-pation. Since God is a personal creator, one tends to think of God as responsible for everything, including so-called natural evil. Is it better that there be no such God? In sum, the size of the evil and the destructive effect on individual persons can wipe out all possible meaning.[24] Process theologies of God that shift classical ideas about God as the fullness of being and limit God's power do not resolve

---

[22] David O'Connor, *God, Evil, and Design: An Introduction to the Philosophi-cal Issues* (Oxford: Blackwell, 2008), 212.

[23] Marilyn McCord Adams, *Horrendous Evils and the Goodness of God* (Ithaca, NY: Cornell University Press, 1999).

[24] Ibid., 26–28.

the problem of evil because it is not an intellectual problem. Evil calls for salvation rather than for God's limitation.

Much of human life consists of avoiding passive and active participation in evil. A catalogue of evils may be needed to push a protected consciousness in the direction of realism. We cannot count or measure evils. Consider the protracted pain involved in a ten-year-old starving to death, and then consider the statistics of that happening in countless individuals in the world at any given time, and proportionately multiply it by the numbers of men, women, and children across the species. We can consider war up close in terms of the carnage of a single battle, the familial misery it causes, and the single loss of a child, and then expand that across history. The list of evils goes on endlessly and ranges in size from cumulative devastation to the physical pain of a single person at any given time. If our sociality means that we cannot be truly happy as a race while so many suffer, some measure of ontic pessimism must be indigenous to human existence. Personal happiness remains at best accidental, episodic, or simply what everyone longs for. Like a black hole, evil acts like a symbol that opens up consciousness to a massive *mysterium iniquitatis*.

So great is the pervasiveness of evil that Christianity developed a doctrine to account for it: original sin. Although it is not necessary here to distinguish between sin and evil, the doctrine seeks to protect God the creator from the charge of being responsible for the apparent perversions of creation. It transfers the power of sin and evil in the world to a morally autonomous force, personified as Satan and evil spirits and perpetrated by human choice. In some classical philosophical accounts of evil it does not exist as an independent power but as a lack or deficiency of being. Whatever exists is good, so that neither finitude nor deficiency of being qualifies as a "something." But this may be a rationalization of what the common noun indicates is substantial. The lack of goodness in the world still implicates God as creator. The damaged condition of our being, inside and outside each one, disallows buying a facile human innocence at the price of minimizing the evil of massive suffering, especially of human beings within socially constructed systems.

A distinction between two dimensions of a consciousness of evil in the world helps to pinpoint more closely the source of cosmic pessimism.[25] One can think of evil in the world in the large terms of social disorders that aggressively attack human life. These are the bias, hatred, or knowing ignorance and neglect of people who are dehumanized by cultural, social, economic, and political systems. These systemic disorders, because they regulate performance that discriminates and kills, take on the character of something objectively evil. Recognizing these patterns in society allows people to react against them and actively strive to construct better systems. This work does mitigate evil in the world; enormous good can be accomplished by fighting social evil in the same way that medicines can fight disease. But there is no end to it. And those who fight social evil are themselves subject to frustration and burnout.

One can also think of evil in terms of the destruction done to each individual human person who is its victim. This microscopic view of evil can be more telling because in it the love of God seems more directly challenged. Consider the effect on the parent of the cruel death of a child. At this point Darwin's faith ran out.

Appreciation of the pervasiveness of evil can lead to cosmic pessimism. It does not arise first on the level of philosophy or as a rational problem. It belongs to the domain of existential consciousness. One factor of this encounter lies in the size, amount, or degree of evil or the character of a direct experience of it. Ordinarily persons can tolerate a little shadow in their lives. We are not speaking here of an analysis of a coherent pessimism that serves as a realist protection from utopian thinking.[26] The pessimism described here flows from encountering the destruction that evil causes and consists of a negative fundamental moral attitude.[27] It refers to a kind of totalizing

---

[25] Ibid., 28–29.

[26] Roger Scruton, *The Uses of Pessimism: And the Danger of False Hope* (Oxford: Oxford University Press, 2010).

[27] The category is drawn from Dietrich von Hildebrand, *Fundamental Moral Attitudes* (New York: Books for Libraries Press, 1969). Here the moral attitude functions negatively, like a vice, to become a basic disposition that colors one's perception of reality.

disposition toward the world. Another factor in the formation of this pessimism lies in the constant unrelenting presence of this evil. One can fight against it, and even make some small inroads, but they remain fragmentary.[28] Evil often seems to have the upper hand and, together with a sense of randomness, it leaves life in this world rudderless. The result of this encounter with evil is scandal. There are of course degrees of cosmic pessimism, but it surrounds everyone as a temptation.

In sum, ontic pessimism today transcends the existentialism of the twentieth century. It refers more strictly to a current historical worldview, influenced by the statistics of poverty, the current pervasiveness and depths of social hatreds, and the natural way in which death-dealing bias becomes invisible, institutionalized routine. Gradually, too, the realization of how thoroughly human civilization is destroying the infrastructure of planetary life itself shrouds everything with an aura of fate. Idealism gradually cedes to different forms of competition and an individualism that sees no other way forward than by seeking short-term, personal, and local goals. This ontic pessimism has more far-reaching effects than can be discerned in an individual's consciousness. It attacks the seriousness or the realism of a theological imagination and tends to portray it as fancy.

The three categories of metaphysical skepticism, relativism, and ontic pessimism set up the structure for introducing the academic discipline of theology. The premise is that theology transcends church catechisms the way biochemistry and medicine transcend public opinion on the best way to address a disease. The categories

---

[28] After encountering the situation of the Middle East firsthand, Barack Obama reflected, "Was it possible that abstract principles and high-minded ideals were and always would be nothing more than a pretense, a palliative, a way to beat back despair, but no match for the more primal urges that really moved us, so that no matter what we said or did, history was sure to run along its predetermined course, an endless cycle of fear, hunger and conflict, dominance and weakness?" (*A Promised Land* [New York: Crown, 2020], 366). He recalled this feeling as occurring after his speech in Cairo in 2009.

are ways of gathering sets of experiences and questions that are addressed in a critical and methodic way by theological reasoning. It is impossible to measure accurately the extent and the depth of these challenges to religious consciousness, and equally difficult to estimate and pinpoint a common interest in theology itself. But it is becoming a necessary pursuit at some level for anyone who wants to participate fully and critically in American culture and in a Christian faith tradition.

Part Two

A Framework for a
Holistic Approach to
Theology

2

Religious Consciousness
in the Face of Skepticism

Theology involves religious consciousness. Social history and cultural evolution help to explain why religious consciousness no longer describes a default mechanism of twenty-first-century Western life. Therefore, theology has to begin with some account of the existential faith that provides the soil in which theology grows. The problem of metaphysical skepticism requires an apologetic framework—theology has to explain itself. In whatever way one defines it, theology has to give some account of transcendent or "religious" experience.

The implied subject matter of this chapter lies buried in a host of related concepts that support the discipline. Christian theology lies nested in some form of communitarian religious consciousness that is defined by the language of faith and revelation. An explanation of the discipline of theology will entail clarifying those terms. Theology also needs to reflect on the epistemology of the object of faith and revelation because the process of knowing defines the character of the discipline. This chapter aims at laying out these defining characteristics in clear terms. But two overarching concepts assume a central importance: the first is a theory of revelation that is broad enough to encompass Christian faith and the faith of other religious traditions; the second is a theory of knowledge that may be called critical and realistic and that accounts for a true but utterly unique form of knowledge.

Religious Experience and Consciousness

Religious experience may be considered what Edward Schillebeeckx called an anthropological constant. This means that phenomenological analysis of human existence uncovers the dynamics of religious experience and accounts for it as a universal possibility across the history of the species.[1] Such an analysis cannot discover a universal form of the religious question, let alone an answer, except in broad abstract terms. But one finds religious response at every juncture of the long road of human history. Without specifying either a definite form or content of religious experience, without claiming its roots drink from personal individual or corporate social experience, and without commentary on its internal truth value, religious experience may be considered a common human phenomenon.

Given the plurality of different religions and religious experiences, this discussion favors the expression *religious consciousness* over *religious experience.* In contrast to religious experience, which seems too definite and focused to match the variety of such occasions, religious consciousness is deliberately open and indefinite. Given the diversity of religious experiences and of religions, it is difficult to determine what exactly a particular religious experience is. The term *religious consciousness* softens and accommodates the deliberate vagueness of the subject matter. It refers all at once to a particular experience of an individual, or a shared community experience, or a type of experience as differentiated from, for example, other kinds of experience and knowledge underlying other academic disciplines.

All religious experiences and thus consciousnesses ultimately take on individual forms. But various social metrics may enable descriptions of the dynamics and certain formal characteristics of religious consciousness. Different descriptions of religious consciousness from within the Western Christian tradition may evoke recognition. Their variety illustrates diversity within a common cultural tradition. Far from being exhaustive, they imply distinctiveness right down to

---

[1] Edward Schillebeeckx, *Christ: The Experience of Jesus as Lord* (New York: Seabury Press, 1980), 740–41.

each religious encounter. Bypassing an adequate phenomenology of what counts as religious experience, a few characteristics of such an experience drawn from the Western Jewish and Christian traditions can distinguish it from the object of aesthetic, moral, poetic, and philosophical discourse.

A religious experience draws one into a sphere of deep, comprehensive meaning and value. "Meaning" here refers to the recognition that some word, object, or proposal makes sense, is understandable or intelligible, so that one identifies it in a larger framework of understanding the world. Meaning is coherent. Adding the words "deep" and "comprehensive" alters things considerably. Deep meaning communicates something more than the practical or functional meaning of a chair as something on which one sits, or food as what one eats. Comprehensive meaning applies to issues as large as life, on a level achieved by Viktor Frankl in the context of the Nazi concentration camps where human life did not count at all.[2] A religious experience calls forth a sphere of the intelligibility of being itself, of my life as a phenomenon, of history, and of existence.

A religious experience opens up an awareness of value, of something important outside of oneself that solicits commitment. Kierkegaard saw this dedication as a higher form of freedom consisting of steadfast loyalty, a freedom that can transcend attraction and assertively construct an inner self. Commitment to religiously experienced value bends it back so that the value communicates itself to the person who embraces it. Abraham Joshua Heschel referred to religious piety as a fundamental and guiding orientation of a person toward something outside the self that orients all one's relationships and gives purpose to life.[3]

John Wesley described religious experience as encountering God within, as a divine presence represented by the symbol "Spirit." He asked how we know for ourselves that we are united

---

[2] Viktor E. Frankl, *Man's Search for Meaning: An Introduction to Logotherapy* (New York: Washington Square Press, 1969). Immanuel Kant recognized in absolute terms that the meaning of a human person cannot be reduced to being an instrument or a thing. Imagine the negation of that truism in a death camp.

[3] Abraham Joshua Heschel, "An Analysis of Piety," *Moral Grandeur and Spiritual Audacity* (New York: Farrar, Straus and Giroux, 1996), 310.

with God in a positive relationship. By the same kind of experience by which one knows that he or she is alive: "By the same immediate consciousness you will know, if your soul is alive to God."[4] Many authors insist on the self-authenticating character of religious experience.

Friedrich Schleiermacher appealed to philosophical analysis of human subjectivity to establish an opening in human consciousness to a subtler account of religious experience.[5] What Schleiermacher later called an experience of absolute dependence refers to a possibility of appreciating that we do not bear within ourselves an explanation for our being, a reason that we usually demand in order to understand everything else. This potential recognition is universally available.[6] Rather than being merely serendipitous, religious consciousness possesses roots in the structure of human existence. Religion cannot be reduced to something useful for society; it has metaphysical grounding within the makeup of human consciousness.

A metaphysical grounding of the potential of religious consciousness does not restrict diversities of religious experiences but demands them. For example, Delores Williams describes American Black women's religious experience as a liberating call to agency in a desert-like situation of racist and hierarchical subjugation. "In the vertical encounter between black women and God in the wilderness experience, transformation of consciousness and epistemological process come together in the new great faith-consciousness this meeting bestows upon black women."[7]

---

[4] John Wesley, "The Witness of the Spirit," *The Works of the Rev. John Wesley,* V (New York: J. & J. Harper, 1826–27), 94.

[5] Friedrich Schleiermacher, *On Religion: Speeches to Its Cultured Despisers* (New York: Harper Torchbooks, 1958), 11–21.

[6] Friedrich Schleiermacher, *The Christian Faith* (London: Bloomsbury T&T Clark, 2016), #4, 12–18.

[7] Delores Williams, "Black Experience, Wilderness Experience, Theological Task," in *Sisters in the Wilderness: The Challenge of Womanist God-Talk* (Maryknoll, NY: Orbis Books, 1993), 159.

Faith

When religious consciousness is transferred into the domain of Christianity, it acquires the names *faith* and *revelation*. Faith refers to the religious reception of the object of religious consciousness, namely, God revealing God's self. Faith and revelation point to two dimensions of a single Christian consciousness. Faith corresponds to a human reception of revelation or to the content received; revelation refers to the process of communication and to what is received. Revelation requires reception to be revelation. Faith also refers to a common human response manifest within other religions or outside them, directed to revelation outside the Jewish and Christian line or to something less than revelation.[8] Although they are two sides of a single phenomenon, we begin with some broad characteristics describing faith, even though theologians may argue whether faith or revelation should be the primary focus of a theological imagination.

Although we speak of an act of faith, faith should not be considered primarily as a particular human act alongside others in the course of a day. More important, faith is a virtue, an inner disposition that enables acts and a commitment that encompasses and orients a person. Faith engages the whole person as a subjective actor. Rather than being elicited by the will, or by the mind exclusively, or arising as a spontaneous feeling, or as a particular mixture of emotions, faith arises out of all of these facets of a person's life. But faith as a virtue points to committed loyalty or a holistic existential response. Virtue suggests a stable moral disposition oriented toward actual responses to values. This framework transfers faith into a more diffuse and comprehensive register of human response. One cannot reduce faith to an assent of the mind, or a determined will to believe, or an affective sentiment. If it is fitting to describe the totality of the individual person as a mysterious reservoir containing untold depths, faith has its source in that well. It is deep enough

---

[8] People confess faith in a remarkable range of things. Dealing with "religious" faith, properly speaking, will require an internal criterion that marks it as religious.

for people to be uncertain of their faith; they have to read it, like a compass, in the pattern of their behavior.

Paul Tillich defined faith as "ultimate concern": "Faith is the state of being ultimately concerned."[9] Each of the two words carries a lesson. The idea of a concern lies open in its scope and suggests intensity. Concern as a human response is attentive, focused, and persistent. Concern picks up a comprehensive intensity that echoes Kierkegaard, who spoke of faith as passionate because it was attached to the transcendent one. Tillich's choice of the term *ultimate* serves a double purpose of correlating the subjective response with its object. Because the object of faith is ultimate, and not one object among others, the attachment to it should respond in kind. Faith runs deep; it centers a person. In the other direction, ultimate concern demands ultimacy. An ultimate concern about anything less than the ultimate would be idolatry in the classic sense of God's command (Ex 20:3–4). Faith in a theological sense, therefore, carries its criterion of authenticity within itself. Faith as a religious response refers to something qualitatively different from many of the things in which people commonly say they have faith. The object of faith can only be the ultimate.

Right below the surface of any discussion of faith today lies the question of its relation to what is called reason. This discussion, as old as Christianity itself, has particular relevance today when the rationalism of the Enlightenment has assumed a new variant in scientism. Yet few scientists would speak of reason devoid of imagination and creativity. Mind as a category contains much more than a narrow concept of reason suggests. Faith takes its place within the reflective power of human existence as a function of the human mind. John Henry Newman showed how faith includes a rational process of informal and spontaneous reasoning that reaches a conclusion and carries an assent that bears its own form of certainty.[10] Paul Tillich, appealing to a different metaphor, describes ecstatic reason.

---

[9] Paul Tillich, *Dynamics of Faith* (New York: Harper and Brothers, 1957), 1.

[10] John Henry Newman, *An Essay in Aid of a Grammar of Assent* (Notre Dame, IN: University of Notre Dame Press, 1979), 270–99.

Conscious mind is drawn beyond itself and stands above itself, not grasping the object of faith, but being grasped by it.[11] An opposition between faith, imagination, and reason collapses in the very effort of the mind to divide itself into non-communicating compartments. Holistic interacting reflection offers a better guide to human rational response. In the end, faith and reason entail each other.

Analysis of another polarity within faith itself helps to clarify the dynamics of faith on both a theoretical and a personal level. On the premise that faith consists of an existential way of standing before ultimate reality, beliefs express the content or object of faith in propositional terms. Various other forms of behavior also express contours of personal faith. For example, a primary indicator of personal faith lies in patterns of action. Consistent behavioral responses reveal basic values and commitments. Beliefs give those commitments linguistic form and express content to what, without them, might appear as "blind" or incoherent. Much more will be said about the way beliefs represent the transcendent object of faith and communicate it on a public level. But it is essential to underline the distinction between faith and the beliefs that put it into words and publicly affirm it. The history of theology can be described as the steady reinterpretation of beliefs as they carry a relatively stable faith commitment into different societies and new linguistically defined cultures. Beliefs are constantly changing, even in the cycle of a personal life, while faith can remain constant.

The distinction between faith and beliefs that consistently interact with each other across the passage of time and the multiplicity of cultures offers a context for discussing another polarity that structures personal faith: faith and doubt. This polarity characterizes both faith and commitment to beliefs but in different ways. The primal response of faith is directed toward "the ultimate," which by definition transcends all finite things that offer themselves to our understanding. More will be said about the quality of one's

---

[11] "We shall call the organ with which we receive the contents of faith 'self-transcending,' or ecstatic, reason. . . . Ecstatic reason is reason grasped by an ultimate concern" (Paul Tillich, *Systematic Theology,* I [Chicago: University of Chicago Press, 1951], 53).

grasp of transcendent reality further on, but at this point, because transcendence by definition lacks immediate empirical evidence, it always appears vulnerable to doubt. Beliefs are even more vulnerable because culture outgrows the linguistic forms of their presentation. But in both areas doubt does not appear entirely negative. It functions as a stimulus for engagement, for injecting faith with courage. Doubt also acts as a positive catalyst for reinterpretation, for bringing beliefs into the parameters of credibility within a contemporary understanding of the world.

To conclude this short introduction to faith, all people live by faith, for some ultimate concern synthesizes every life and constitutes its coherence. What differs among people is the object of their faith, what they set as their ultimate. But the ultimate cannot appear as something readily available; Christian theology considers God to be the object of revelation. An adequate response to metaphysical skepticism must contain some account of a theological conception of revelation.

The Structure of Revelation

Metaphysical skepticism has more problems with revelation than it does with faith. Many disenchanted people admit that they live by some kind of faith, but its object often takes the form of a commitment to humanity or trust in the power of reason. Nowhere does this sentiment prevail more than within the university. For theology to qualify as an academic discipline, it has to give an account of its subject matter and the source of its knowledge. Christian theology calls this revelation.

Philosopher of religion John Smith offers a relatively straightforward theory of revelation that has potential for describing in a formal way the source of both Christian and other traditions of faith. As a general theory, it will look a bit different in each of its applications. But a general conception of revelation will go some way toward enabling a conversation between different religious traditions. According to Smith's analysis, religious revelation has a threefold logical pattern: "There is the divine reality to be disclosed, there is the medium of disclosure, and there is the interpreter who reads the meaning of the disclosure in terms of the medium."[12] The three elements provide an outline that describes the structure of revelation and a possible framework for specific conversations across religious traditions.

First, the object of revelation correlates with "the ultimate" of Tillich's theology of faith; in Christian theology, God is revealed. God is not available to empirical perception. The basic problem of Christian revelation thus stems from the transcendence of God. But the revelation of God still has to be understood in historical terms. Revelation points to a historical question rather than the logical or philosophical problem of whether one can prove the existence of God. Revelation signifies a historical disclosure of God. Such an encounter with God would be unintelligible if it did not correlate with human experience or some actual religious consciousness. While clearly not the same as knowing empirical data, revelation cannot be totally dissimilar from other forms of knowing. Revelation has to be explained not by a suspension but by an intensification of human capabilities. One has to appeal to human experience, language, and thought to interpret what is going on in the historical revelation of God.

Second, the distinctive character of a religious revelation resides in its mediated character. Revelation consists of an event in history. This means that from a human perspective revelation cannot be planned; it happens occasionally rather than being readily available. Rather than the product of research or inference, revelation refers to what cannot be discovered by abstract reason, or derived from a general theory, or anticipated, or deduced. The historical character of revelation also entails that it takes place through a historical medium. Because God transcends the world, awareness of God must be mediated through something of the world that is other than God. "The 'something else' is the *medium* through which God, who is not a sensible object, is to be known if known at all."[13] Such media

---

[12] John E. Smith, "The Disclosure of God and Positive Religion," in *Experience and God* (New York: Oxford University Press, 1968), 92.

[13] Ibid., 71n.

of revelation as they appear in the Bible comprise persons, such as prophets; or events, such as the liberation from Egypt; or things, such as the Ark of the Covenant, or derivatively the written word of God; or the order of nature and its awesome constellations. The media of revelation determine the character of a particular revelation. In other words, what is disclosed through revelation cannot be gained in some other way; it is historical and initially tied to the medium of its disclosure.[14]

Smith expands the concept of a medium of a revelation of God. A medium is a finite reality bearing the divine presence and pointing beyond itself. Any reality may serve as a medium of the divine presence in principle, because God, as creator, is related to all things and all things depend on God. A medium of revelation both makes God present and points beyond itself to God as other than itself and transcendent. The medium is not God but discloses God. The medium thus bears a dialectical character; it is not the divine but leads the imagination beyond itself to God. A medium thus entails both reciprocity and a gap between itself and its object; the medium reveals the presence of God but does not take the place of God, which would be idolatrous. The medium discloses God by bearing the divine presence but remains distinct from God in the process.[15]

Smith illustrates the dialectical mode in which media communicate through the example of interpersonal communication.[16] The dynamics of the revelation of one self to another and the knowledge gained from such a self-revelation offers an analogy for understanding the revelation of God. An analysis of the concealed character of the inner self in the physical presence of another, and the use of external language and gesture by an individual to communicate the self to the other, sets up a way of understanding the mechanism of

---

[14] Ibid., 73.

[15] This paragraph is drawn directly from Smith (ibid., 77–80). It may be noted that Smith's characterization of a medium bears a close resemblance to Paul Tillich's description of a symbol. See *Dynamics of Faith*, 41–54, where Tillich uses symbol to describe the language of faith. See also Roger Haight, *Dynamics of Theology* (Maryknoll, NY: Orbis Books, 2001), 129–66.

[16] What follows paraphrases Smith, "The Disclosure of God and Positive Religion," 83–87.

historical revelation. The self as subject communicates itself to the other person by expressing itself in and through the media. Even though the self can never be fully represented by the media, because they can never catch up with the mysterious inner self, still they enable self-communication directly but not immediately. The self will always be more than the media that render it "objective" or public.

The third leg of the structure of revelation consists of interpretation of the media by those who encounter them. In the beginning, this refers to the first responders to a mediated revelation; later, the interpreters are the community and those who in effect represent the community. Revelation requires interpreters who read the media and historical signs of God's presence and make explicit for the community the meaning and relevance of the mediation at any given time. Such is the task of the prophets in scripture and the theologians in later receiving communities.[17] As representatives of the community, their interpretation cannot be merely personal in the sense of "individual"; it must so represent the community that in effect the community takes part in the process of interpretation.

Smith's theory of the structure of revealed religions correlates closely with Christianity, and he uses Christianity to illustrate his proposal. But the theory in its rudimentary form has wider application and provides a basis for "first-level" comparisons between religions. But faith traditions are living things that are always in motion, so this structure has to be seen as a schema for a flexible, ongoing process.

Transcendence and Immanence

Metaphysical skepticism often stems from the language and beliefs of popular religion. Critics of religion not versed in theology may be directing their reproach to naive rather than reflective religious language. It is more appropriate to discuss criticism of religion in the considered terminology that the discipline of theology provides.

---

[17] Ibid., 87–92.

An example of this is found in the formal question of "where" God is located by the imagination. Freud imagined God as nonexistent, a projection of need and desire. More positively, others think God is so transcendent that our words never reach their object. Theories of projection hold that the word *God* is a stand-in for human ideals or the authority that society imposes. Some reject the idea of God because it undermines human autonomy in thinking and responsibility in acting. Believers may think of God as a friendly, cooperating, and finally saving partner in life. All such thinking tacitly presupposes God as a person or substance other than ourselves, out there, but somehow impinging upon, if not intervening in, the processes of nature and one's own life.

The conversation about God would be different if God were conceived as a dimension immanent to all reality, within the world and the human subject rather than "over against" them. The merging of God transcendent and God immanent, then, throws bright light on the flawed logic of everyday speech by changing presuppositions of speaking about God that are taken for granted. A reflective critique of ordinary religious language applied to the terms of transcendence and immanence changes implicit suppositions about God's accessibility to human experience.[18]

The transcendence and the immanence of God are both logically distinct and identical.[19] Logically, the transcendence of God indicates that God "goes beyond" all limits. God is infinite. But *transcendent* does not mean "up there," or "distant," as if God were an object or a personal subject like a human being. No place holds God; God does not rest in a location; God is not subject to or contained by space or time. God subsists beyond the limits of all physical and finite reality, not in the sense of being "outside" them, but in being other than anything imaginable. These affirmations about God are indescribable; they transcend all that can be imagined because they refer to God.

---

[18] The discussion of the transcendence and immanence of God remains phenomenological at this point. The theological underpinnings of this aspect of God will be addressed in Chapter 5 in terms of the theology of creation.

[19] This reflection draws on John J. Thatamanil, "Reimagining Immanence," in *The Immanent Divine* (Minneapolis: Fortress Press, 2006), 174–201.

Because transcendence means that no place holds God, so that God would be out there or anywhere, it follows that the transcendence of God is not contrary to God's immanence. The contrast presupposes putting God somewhere, in a place. The transcendence of God thus actually entails God's immanence to all finite reality. The immanence of God flows from God's not being a thing, something that can be bound by limits that identify it by distinction or specification. A better metaphor for God's immanence than "being within" might be an undefined energy that suffuses, saturates, and encompasses all reality. A first conclusion can be drawn from this mutuality between the transcendence and immanence of God: God is not located outside the self as though God were an object. God is found within the self because God infinitely transcends the self and pervades all that is.

The basic move of the mind to help approach God's transcendent immanence subverts the idea that God can be imagined as a being at all. Rather than a substance, one can think of God as an act, a verb, an activity, or a dynamism that does not have boundaries that would make it an object. Thinking of God as pure activity, without a subject acting but as the dynamism itself, does not allow one to fix God in the imagination as *a being*, but creates an intentional framework for positing God as a reality that is simultaneously transcendent and immanent by its ubiquitous action. God is not a something, and not a person, since the definite article implies limiting boundaries. The symbol of "pure action" allows one to construct the unity of God with the finite world in a new way. God as act provides the intrinsic power of everything that exists. Nothing can exist without the sustaining ground that supports it. There can be no separability between something that exists and the energy that sustains it, between heat and agent-fire.[20] A second conclusion can be drawn about the reciprocity of God's immanence and transcendence: it is

---

[20] Describing God as activity, Joseph Bracken writes: "The grounding activity is not an entity, and the entity is other than the grounding activity. At the same time they are not-two since only together, namely, as grounding activity and that which exists in virtue of the grounding activity, are they one concrete reality" (Joseph Bracken, "Infinity and the Logic of Non-Dualism," *Hindu-Christian Studies Bulletin* 11 [1998]: 41).

facilitated by thinking of God not as a substance but as dynamic action or energy. Theological language transcends anthropomorphism.

The dynamic simultaneity and identity of the transcendence and immanence of God to the world help to explain a paradox of religious consciousness. People do not "meet" God as an object over against the self, even when the imagination so depicts it. Rather, as the mystics insist, the "place" where people contact God lies within self-consciousness. True, a religious experience entails transcendence: what is experienced is other than the self. At the same time, this transcendence may be experienced as constituting the self, as the analysis of Schleiermacher in the previous chapter indicated. This means that the action of God both constitutes us, and thus is a constituent part of us, while remaining completely other than us. "Dynamic non-dualism" means that the transcendence of God intrinsically constitutes the world and each element of it by the intrinsic action of its presence.[21]

A third conclusion may be drawn here: the transcendence and immanence of God indicate paradoxical characteristics of religious consciousness; people who are drawn into God's presence, or experience God's power, "participate" in God. But that which one encounters in religious consciousness cannot be reduced to the self. This paradox will help in responding to the problem of faith as knowledge. It stimulates an analysis that helps to explain the language of John Wesley when he maintained that he had sure knowledge of what he experienced within himself.

Faith as Personal and Communicable

The immanence and transcendence of the object of faith correlates with another tension that describes the character of faith and helps to clarify the domain of theology. Faith refers to an intimate and comprehensive human response. Its personal character partly explains the privatization of religious sentiment that prevails today. Yet, despite the individually personal character of faith, faith is still

---

[21] Thatamanil, *The Immanent Divine*, 184–86.

communicable and able to hold communities together. How do these two dimensions interact with each other?

Faith, when it is considered existentially as a human disposition, defines the self. Another way of stating this comes down to sheer description: the ways persons assume responsibility for themselves, orient their lives, and constitute themselves practically define their basic faith. So each person's faith is distinctive. But this does not add up to individualism. No historian would minimize the role of the community in faith; each person's faith rises up through a community or a set of communities. But as important as external stimuli are, personal faith cannot be reduced to the influence of the community, because faith always has an inner dimension that also allows for criticism of the community or departure from it.[22]

Consider the relationship between one's personal faith and that of others, whether within the same community of faith or of different faith traditions. This relationship can be illuminated by two principles. The first recalls the fact that two distinct sets of influence shape the identity of each person—one stemming from one's inner resources, the other from the physical and social situations that intrinsically contribute to personhood. In a sense, then, each person has two sources and dimensions of the self: the autonomous self, which refers to our agency; and our social self, our action as a member of various groups that we allow to shape our inner selves or that did so in early life. These intermingled relationships show how the deep personal character of faith, across communities and religious traditions, never amounts to solipsism. Faith is a dynamic response to reality that has roots in a community and draws from experiences of the world outside the self and yet remains a function of the autonomous self.

The second principle flows from the transcendent character of the object of faith. The content of faith reveals itself as being other than the self and thus relevant to others, potentially to all. In other words, the transcendence of the object of faith manifests a wider relevance than merely to the self. The transcendent value of the object

---

[22] Wilfred Cantwell Smith, *The Meaning and End of Religion* (New York: Mentor Books, 1964), 158–60.

of faith also exerts pressure to be communicated. The plurality of faiths may frustrate that impulse, and that will be discussed in the next chapter. But in the light of transcendence any idea of an object of faith that is exclusively mine makes no sense.

The intensely personal character of faith raises the question of how it can be communicated. This question has to be considered in the light of the distinction between faith and belief made earlier. Faith is an existential self-disposition, both of a person and deriva-tively of a community. Beliefs arise out of faith, that is, faith gives rise to self-expressive beliefs, but they are not identical with faith and always are relative to culture. As W. C. Smith explains, the cumulative tradition of beliefs is the result of the faith of people in the past that actually causes the faith of people in the present.[23] This may seem dismissive; in fact, it illustrates the essential elements of how personal faith is communicable.

One can apprehend the content of faith of others and other tradi-tions by analogy through its expressions. Deep personal engagement with art, with fundamental human entanglements of love and anger, of joy, tragedy, and loss, and personal commitment to political ideals like justice and the commonweal, can be communicated across these common categories of human experiences by analogy. This is more readily possible among people who share a formal and deliberate religious consciousness and commitment than among those who find no resonance in it. But fundamental human experiences of the most personal kind can be shared in some measure. Smith does not propose the ease of genuine communication; he calls the process of knowing another's faith an inference that is accompanied by interpretation through imaginative sympathy, which is disciplined by intellectual rigor, and checked by elaborate historical procedures and criticism.[24] That adds up to humanistic resonance and reflective analysis. A common formal structure of faith allows people to ap-proach the content of another faith tradition by analogy.

To sum up here, the profoundly personal character of faith and its communicability, so that it may function as a bond of a community,

---

[23] Ibid., 168.
[24] Ibid., 169.

have to be held together as two dimensions of a single human reaction and disposition. This tensive unity in its turn sheds explanatory light on the phenomenon of two basically different conceptions of Christian theology. Some theologians approach the discipline "outside in," while others approach it "inside out." The outside-in theologian looks to the history of the expressions of faith across the tradition, especially at its early normative scriptural statement, to determine the essential content of faith. The inside-out theologian looks at the genetic structure of faith and, with the distinction of beliefs and faith in mind, focuses on the existential faith behind the doctrines and practices of history that express the faith, and brings that commitment forward in language appropriate to the culture being addressed. An understanding of the simultaneous and mutually related dimensions of faith can be used to legitimate both of these theological trends.

The Cognitive Character and Truth of Faith

A response to metaphysical skepticism has to address the question of whether people of faith really know something that others do not. Does theology represent something real beyond subjective reactions? There are many ways of knowing. Poetic knowledge need not be reduced to factual knowledge in order to be true; descriptive sociological generalizations offer qualified truths that depend upon data gathering and are subject to interpretation. Faith knowledge is *sui generis*, distinct from all other kinds. But its formal claim to truth requires more analysis.

Dionysius the Areopagite is a key figure in Eastern and Western mystical knowledge.[25] He threads his way from apophaticism, the idea that nothing positive can be said about God, to a sense of being in contact with God negatively, in a way transcending all other

---

[25] The reference is to Pseudo-Dionysius the Areopagite, a Syrian theologian born in the fifth century CE who assumed the name of the convert of Paul in Athens (Acts 17:34) and wrote contemplative theology. Later translated into Latin, his writings were influential in medieval theology. The reference here is to his short treatise "The Mystical Theology," http://hoye.de/theo/denistext.pdf.

forms of knowledge. One knows that what one encounters cannot be reduced to anything that appears to represent it. What Dionysius calls mystical bears direct relevance to the epistemology of faith and theology in a number of respects. First, a genuine religious consciousness of God is simultaneously an unknowing knowing; the perception of faith-consciousness includes the awareness that the transcendent infinitely exceeds comparability to anything we know in this world. Second, real knowledge of God subsists in that negation; by denying any similarity with this-worldly knowledge, the mind actually has "ascended" into transcendence because it implicitly recognizes the limitations of finitude.[26] Third, the dynamics of faith may be described as discovering the transcendent in finite media as that infinity which exceeds and constitutes finitude itself. Reciprocally, the dynamics of revelation may be described as being led into a transcendent sphere through finite media.

Reflective analysis proposes faith knowledge as affirmation of a simultaneously unknown transcendence through and in the finite concrete media and conceptual names or predicates. In knowledge of God, the mind ascends, *through* sensible perceptions; the mind is raised aloft into the unknown. The metaphor of ecstasy or ecstatic reason communicates the idea of being united with divine presence, but as an absolute unknown, as darkness. The spiritual freedom of mind reaches beyond the finite. What do we know about God? Nothing. Yet a positive affirmation arises out of the unknowing and expresses a recognized contact with something transcendent and ineffable.

The negation is not one of opposition, but of transcendence: an affirmation of something absolutely above or beyond, and thus not contrastive. The encounter with transcendence impels the necessity to deny that any this-worldly meanings can be predicated of God in an isomorphic way. If worldly language described God, it would reduce God to the finite meaning of the medium and fail at mediating the transcendent. Faith knowledge of God involves an essential paradox and dialectical tension. God becomes manifested in the very negation that anything we say of God applies, because

---

[26] Ibid., 1.2.

the God we have encountered completely transcends the predication or assignment of meaning. God's infinity breaks open limits
and is recognized in the aura of absolute mystery. The dialectical
character of language about God means that the negation does not
disappear in the affirmation of God's goodness, mercy, and love.[27]

Friedrich Schleiermacher described another way of looking at the
mediated character of religious consciousness. The consciousness of
being in relation to God is always framed by an experience of being
in relation to the world.[28] The inseparability of being in relation to
God and in the world account for the inescapable anthropomorphic
dimensions of religious language. Theology seeks to distinguish
the object of faith from its mode of representation in spontaneous
speech.[29] But a sensible imagination is always in play. Fixed squarely
in the physical world, religious consciousness can never have a
direct or immediate knowledge of God. Ecstasy does not literally
describe religious consciousness but metaphorically evokes what
Tillich called clinging to God over an abyss of nonbeing, and Karl
Rahner called encountering absolute incomprehensible mystery.
In the end, one has to admit that religious knowledge cannot be
adequately portrayed in objective terms.

Internally, religious consciousness readily appears to be self-
authenticating. But more can be said about personal and social
verification. This idea operates within an existential humanistic
rather than a measurable empirical framework. A long fruitful life
accompanied by a religious consciousness accumulates credibility
and conviction for the individual across a series of developments and
changes of specific beliefs. And an ancient and still vital faith tradition bears evidential witness to its congruity with human existence.

In sum, Christian theology's response to metaphysical skepticism
claims that faith can generate real knowledge. This knowledge transpires within the framework of a critical symbolic realism. Criticism

---

[27] This means we affirm things of God knowing that we do not know what
we are talking about. We know, according to Thomas Aquinas, that God is, but
we do not and cannot really know what God is positively, but only through
negation, knowing what God is not.

[28] Schleiermacher, *The Christian Faith*, #5, #30.

[29] Ibid., #5.

refers to the highly reflective character of theological analysis that describes the working of a religious imagination. The concept of a symbol correlates precisely with the mediated character of all awareness of a transcendent "object." Like Smith's medium, "symbol" refers to an object, event, or concept that communicates something other than itself. A symbol mediates; it both refers to that "other" and renders it present. Rather than referring to an attenuated form of knowledge, symbol expands the range of human perception: symbols open up new dimensions of reality. The functions of mediation and critique add up to realism: an analysis of knowledge that shows a real intentional contact with what is known. Experiential faith knowledge of God is real because God is within the human subject and has an immanent resonance within the human mind that knows itself as being affected by transcendence.[30]

Faith knowledge grounds theology; theology has no other foundation. Other pseudo-foundations, such as authority in its various sources, or reasoned argument in its various forms, can ultimately be reduced to mediated religious experience and consciousness. Theology does not consist of a body of accumulated objective knowledge that takes its place within a larger body of knowledge based on other more or less verifiable empirical evidence. Such simple but rampant confusion turns theology into "deficient knowledge," judged so by a fundamental mistake in "categories" or kinds of knowledge. Catherine Keller captures the continuous ongoing theological project. With Dionysius she maintains that theology cannot objectify human encounter with God. Theology continually calls established theological language into question and searches for more adequate and accurate communicative terms. "Speaking the divine wisdom in a mystery, theology remains a work of human speech."[31]

---

[30] The language of existential encounter complicates the phrase *objective knowledge,* because the latter would negate its being knowledge of transcendent reality. God is not an object. Thus, if one substituted the word *Dharma* for *God* (in the sentence above beginning with "Experiential faith knowledge of God is real . . . "), many Buddhists would agree.

[31] Catherine Keller, *On the Mystery: Discerning God in Process* (Minneapolis: Fortress Press, 2008), 17.

The response to metaphysical skepticism has to be one of faith. In fact, a firm metaphysical skepticism describes a position based on faith. One cannot escape faith relative to the mysteries that surround human existence. Some faith in the character of ultimate reality based on some historical revelation is the default position of human existence itself. If not faith in God, some other positive form of ultimate reality shapes the intelligibility of empirical reality and its value and destiny. Even agnosticism is a chosen form of faith. The question of faith in transcendent reality thus takes the form of a wager between faiths in ultimate meaning or in ultimate vacuity.

3

Pluralism and Learning
from Other Faiths

Of the three challenges to Christian faith and theology, namely, skepticism, relativism, and pessimism, relativism cuts most deeply. It effectively holds that the quest for ultimacy its illusory. What is more obvious than the profuse diversity of religions, all of them passionately negating one another? Active hostility between religions also factors into the temptation to dismiss the claims of all. Relativism compounds the reaction of metaphysical skepticism.

The problem of relativism seems to be built into the historical character of faith and revelation. All faith and revelation arise out of particular historical experiences. The experience and reception of revelation may reflect a transcendental human desire, but faith's commitment is always historically distinctive. Religious consciousness is founded on a particular event, person, or medium of history. To put it paradoxically, the transcendental structure of religious consciousness ties it to historical mediation. The content of faith cannot be completely lifted out of particular historical media.

But, at the same time, one can argue against relativism on the basis of a common humanity. Universal aspects of the human turn up as historical constants. One can contend that the bond of all religious consciousness to history and to particular experiences does not necessarily lead to relativism: many common beliefs transcend religious boundaries. This chapter makes a case against relativism and for a notion of pluralism in which differentiated faith traditions share a commonality that allows them to understand and enter into conversation with one another. What is important here, more than the claim, are the reasons for this position.

The second goal of this discussion is to show that, even though faith traditions may differ, they can, through mutual understanding and dialogue, learn from one another. One has to be clear here: the beliefs of distinct faith traditions really differ from one another; their mediated contents are not the same. The project is not assimilation but conversation. It is a long global walk from religious wars to reciprocal religious enlightenment, and the baby steps in this direction are undertaken mainly by religious scholars. Comparative theology is part of the theological landscape today. Understanding the structure of Christian theology in a way that allows this to go forward opens up a relatively new critical appropriation of the discipline.

Another reason motivates the discussion of relativism and the diversity of religious consciousness before a constructive discussion of the content of Christian theology. Relativism is toxic; it undermines the possibility of finding ultimate meaning and committing to a consistent religious faith. Arguing against relativism toward a pluralistic religious consciousness turns to a historical consciousness that is positive, generative, and constructive. Historical consciousness can be understood in a way that does not threaten faith but creatively promotes it. A faith consciousness that lacks a sense of historicity, diversity, and new possibility does not correspond with reality. Religious pluralism represents a potentially positive dimension of human existence today.

The discussion of this large topic in a short space moves forward by stages. The first point shows why religious pluralism cannot be avoided; it is necessary and good. But to be pluralism and not merely plurality, requires theory. Is there a framework for discussing diverse faith traditions as comparable? The second section asserts that despite its contentious reception, John Hick's theory of religious pluralism offers a framework for conversation. In its light, the third section offers a more pointed framework for Christian self-understanding while coexisting with other faith traditions. Based on these premises as a starting point, the next three sections consider very broadly the structure of Jewish, Muslim, and Buddhist faith traditions in order to indicate that positive lessons for Christian faith can be learned from them. These analytical historical interpretations also serve as illustrations of how openness to and positive appreciations of other faith traditions can nourish Christian self-understanding. The final section summarizes the discussion against relativism and for a positive appreciation of a self-conscious pluralistic religious situation as the context for Christian theology.

The Necessity of Pluralism

The opposite of relativism is not a single perception of the truth about ultimate reality that can be universally shared. Historical consciousness rules this out, not metaphysically but practically. It was indicated in Chapter 1 that the sociology of knowledge has shown that all knowledge is personally and socially perspectival. Broadly speaking, each culture has its particular conditioned view of the whole of reality, while smaller social groups refine still more narrowly distinct perspectives. It remains true that several factors seem to rule out the ability to communicate and come to some agreement across the boundaries of cultural systems of understanding and mutual disagreements among persons. Many barriers prevent easy communication. But pluralism means that even sharply different conceptions of ultimate reality share formal axes of communication and analogous ways of mutual appreciation, as distinct from exact agreement, that together make up a field of possible communion among faith traditions.

The affirmation of pluralism over against relativism puts pluralism in a positive light. It subverts the radically negative implications of illusion that relativism casts upon all religious belief. But from inside a particular religious conviction, pluralism still appears to be negative. It certainly calls into question the absolute and comprehensive character of particular faith traditions and thus opens up insecurity and doubt. The depth of an intensely held faith often resists in principle other religious worldviews. This first section addresses this problem: given that the religious imagination rejects relativism, what allows and encourage believers to open up their perspectives on religious truth to an appreciation of other faith traditions? What stretches the religious imagination from the fact of religious plurality and diversity to a positive recognition that other faith traditions carry truths that cannot be found within one's own?

Several reasons have already been posited that point in this direction. The theory of the structure of faith and revelation is meant to describe a common human possibility. The threefold configuration of object, medium, and interpretation may not fit the indigenous form or language of every religion equally well. As a formal structure it does not offer either a reductive or an adequate descriptive account. But it points to a common framework that allows a comparison between one's own faith tradition and what is going on analogously, yet perhaps quite differently, in other traditions. As a theory it offers a way of imagining what is going on in other religions, even while remaining subject to the corrections that dialogue provides.

Looking through the lens of that structure, one can imagine that other religious traditions are based on some experience of ultimate reality, whether or not it is called transcendent. The connotations of terms like *ultimate, transcendent,* and *absolute* vary considerably, and theology has to be attentive to particular nuances. But the very existence of a faith tradition assumes that the object of religious consciousness impinges on human awareness. How that is explained would be different in every historical faith tradition.

Consciousness of ultimacy means in some sense that ultimate reality has been internalized or appropriated. The ultimate is experienced; the transcendent is immanent to consciousness; the absolute has affected or made an impression on human consciousness. The descriptive and theoretical variations on such an existential encounter will vary considerably in different traditions, but they may be compared and contrasted meaningfully. It seems self-evident that any reference to the content of revelatory experience will have a mediated character. Content depends on comprehensible mediating language.

Finally, the ultimate, transcendent, or absolute character of the object of religious consciousness opens up the category of mystery. The multiplicity of religious traditions joined with the transcendence or ultimacy of their objects invites the recognition that no single revelation or faith can exhaust the absolute mystery of reality. Rarely do religious faith traditions claim that their beliefs fully comprehend the universe. These dimensions of the religious imagination, which may be verified in some measure within all faith traditions, open up the possibility of religious pluralism having a positive character. They also stimulate a certain curiosity about other religious traditions.

Religious pluralism is necessary because we live in history. Historical consciousness entails the fact that all experience is local and particular, religious experience not excepted. The mediation that makes the object of religious affection more clearly conscious and gives it content will be different for different peoples; interpretation is always perspectival; and the transcendence of the religious object invites humility and the possibility of other true perspectives. The necessity of religious pluralism thus derives from historicity. As far as we can tell today, it represents the natural condition of human existence.

The Possibility of Interfaith Dialogue

The possibility of interfaith dialogue depends on a positive understanding of religious pluralism. One has to have a conception of how various religions relate to one another as a framework for their positive interaction.

John Hick, a philosopher of religion, offers a straightforward descriptive theory of religious pluralism.[1] Hick is a realist; the object of religion is divine reality, also called the eternal one or the real, who is conceived by some as personal and by others as impersonal. In either case, the eternal one is transcendent but also immanent and makes its presence felt on human beings. It is "infinite and is in its fullness beyond the scope of human thought and language and experience; and yet . . . it impinges upon mankind and is encountered

---

[1] John Hick (1922–2012) first offered his theory of religious pluralism in the 1970s and refined it in the course of his career, but the basic structure remained stable. The source for this representation is John Hick, "God Has Many Names," in *God Has Many Names* (Philadelphia: Westminster Press, 1980), 40–59. His theory is best understood as descriptive analysis rather than a representation of the groundwork of religion.

and conceptualized and expressed and responded to in the limited ways which are possible to our finite human nature."[2]

Why is there a plurality of religions rather than one that accommodates and reinforces a single human race? To respond to this question Hick takes a principle from the theory of knowledge of Thomas Aquinas: "The thing known is in the knower according to the mode of the knower."[3] He appropriately extends this principle to the sociology of knowledge: one knows according to the conditioning of one's culture and social situation.

Another factor in religious pluralism is moral, involving religious freedom. Religious experience does not elicit a robotic but a free and discerning reaction. Faith is reflective religious response. "What we call faith is the interpretative element in the religious way of experiencing the world and our lives within it. And faith is an act of cognitive freedom and responsibility. . . . [This means that] the cognitive mode of the knower is largely under the knower's own control. He is able to shut out what he does not want."[4]

Hick offers a Kantian distinction between knowing something as it is "absolutely" or "in itself," and knowing it in its relationship to the self as knower. We can never know God as God is in God's self, but only in God's relationship to the knower. This means that God takes on different forms in the many different relationships in which the transcendent one appears to human beings. "The divine presence is the presence of the Eternal One to our finite human consciousness, and the human projections are the culturally conditioned images and symbols in terms of which we concretize the basic concept of deity."[5] God is recognized within historical and cultural frameworks. The general awareness of God, God pressing

---

[2] Ibid., 42.

[3] Thomas Aquinas, *Summa Theologiae*, II-II, 1.2.

[4] Hick, *God Has Many Names*, 50.

[5] Ibid., 53. "And, in short, we are so formed by the tradition into which we were born and in which we were raised that it is for us unique and absolute and final. Yet I believe that when we accept the fact of religious pluralism we have to learn to refrain from converting that psychological absoluteness into a claim to the objective absoluteness and superiority of our own faith in comparison with all others" (ibid., 57).

in on human consciousness, always takes concrete form from the historical cultural factors that shape human consciousness.

> When I say in a summarizing slogan that God has many names, I mean that the Eternal One is perceived within different human cultures under different forms, both personal and non-personal, and that from these different perceptions arise the religious ways of life which we call the great world faiths. The practical upshot of this thesis is that people of the different religious traditions are free to see one another as friends rather than as enemies or rivals.[6]

Hick's theory of religious pluralism incited many critical reactions, frequently because his theory was misinterpreted materially as a reductive theology rather than a description of how corporate religious faith traditions operate. Hick's theory of religious pluralism correlates fairly well with John Smith's theory of revealed religion. At several junctures one can see the elements of Smith's theory of revelation and faith at work in Hick's description of the experience of God, or, in realist terms, the reception and appropriation of God's influence on human consciousness.

Christian Theology of Religions

Christianity began as a part of Judaism, from which it gradually divided. It came to think of itself in supersessionist terms as the successor to the promises of Abraham and the partner in a new covenant. For centuries Christian theology supported the claim of possessing God's final and absolute revelation to humankind and a doctrine of Christian supremacy: it was the one true religion. As a result of historical developments and for several reasons many Christians no longer share these exclusivist beliefs, and throughout the world Christian churches are developing new relationships with other faith traditions. In a religiously pluralistic world, Christianity

---

[6] Ibid., 59.

has to formulate some basic ideas, if they are not yet adequately developed in various churches, about the way it should situate itself among the plurality of faith traditions that now live together in the major capitals of the world. This means that Christian theology has to accommodate more than the fact of other faiths and revelations. It does not seem possible that theology can ignore the many ancient and vital faith traditions that shape the worldviews by which masses of people reflectively direct their lives.

During the last quarter of the twentieth century the question of the relationship of Christianity to other religions became intense. A number of typologies appeared that attempted to sort out the different stances toward other faith traditions advocated by the churches and theologians. One of the simplest and broadest of these overarching schemas has also been the most tenacious. It divides the basic position, defined stance, or attitude toward other religions into three large categories named exclusivist, inclusivist, and pluralist.[7] These types are useful for comparing and contrasting various ideas; they are also subtle and sometimes deceptive in the different theological visions they bind together. The three types remain creative in stimulating thought. Here they provide an introduction to and a comparative context for a pluralist framework of thinking.[8]

Exclusivist doctrines or attitudes toward other non-Christian faith traditions deny them a role in God's economy of ultimate human salvation, a position that belongs exclusively to Christian faith. Salvation may be attained in no other name than Jesus, who is the Christ. There are different ways of arguing this position and even some mitigation of what seems to be an extremist view today. But the essential theological conviction underlying exclusivism

---

[7] See Alan Race, *Christians and Religious Pluralism: Patterns in the Christian Theology of Religions* (London: SCM Press, 1983).

[8] Types are creations of their authors and users. There are many typologies of the theological positionings of Christian belief relative to other faith traditions, and even typologies of the different ways of assembling the types according to method, content, Christologies, promotion of dialogue, and so on. A more expansive and nuanced typology may be found in Paul Knitter, *Introducing Theologies of Religion* (Maryknoll, NY: Orbis Books, 2002). But this field has continued to race forward since its publication twenty years ago.

assigns to the church—and being a member of it—the central role in human destiny.

An inclusivist has a more expansive view of who are included within the divine economy of salvation. The inclusivist focuses on Jesus Christ but sees his efficacy as objectively opening up salvation to all and potentially including all people no matter what their faith tradition. This expansive view is Christocentric; whether people know it or not, all are saved through the work of Jesus Christ, even before he appeared in history.

By contrast with these two Christian self-understandings in relation to other faith traditions, the pluralist regards the range of faith traditions as potentially bearers of God's revelation and salvation. This does not bless everything about every religion, but it does move the imaginative framework from Christocentrism to theocentrism. The position tends toward a view of religions without ranking, if not egalitarian, or at least not judgmental about the objective superiority of one tradition over another. This clears the way toward an evenhandedness in the dialogue that is ruled out in principle by Christian supremacy.

Evenhandedness can be illustrated for Christian theology by considering the foundational *status quaestionis* in interfaith conversation. Within the framework of the preponderant history of Christian thought, the natural tendency has been to ask whether Christianity is the only true religion or whether there are many.[9] Schubert Ogden spontaneously poses the question that way because persons of each faith will enter the conversation from their particular sense of authenticity. But if all the participants in a conversation are not open to considering the norms of others, the gains of mutual understanding will not move forward to actual learning.[10] Interfaith dialogue requires on the part of each participant an a priori recognition of the

---

[9] Schubert Ogden, *Is There Only One True Religion or Are There Many?* (Dallas: Southern Methodist University Press, 1992).

[10] Comparative theology has to extend beyond a search for similarities between faith traditions. One does not learn as much from similarities as one may from differences. Once some level of communication has been achieved, the way to learning more from different faiths about the human relationship with ultimate reality may be opened up by contrast rather than by assimilation.

distinctive and non-reducible integrity of the religious convictions of the other parties, not as initially judged by one's own criteria. That judgment can only come later.

Edward Schillebeeckx formulated the dialogical question for Christianity in noncompetitive terms. The problem is "How can Christianity maintain its own identity and uniqueness and at the same time attach a positive value to the difference of religions in a non-discriminatory sense?"[11] This rephrasing implies more than it actually states. It presupposes the reality of a revelation and an authenticity of faith in the other tradition. It recognizes the asymmetry between revelations so that, recalling Dionysius, they cannot be compared on the surface of their literal meanings. Faith traditions are embedded in cultures and refer to transcendence. The historical particularity gives each faith tradition a certain autonomy. Interfaith dialogue, therefore, becomes noncompetitive rather than debate. And what is sought in the dialogue is the difference from one's own position so that something may be learned. The plurality of faith traditions thus becomes a good because there is more religious truth in many religions than in any single one.[12]

This fundamental reflection from a Christian standpoint on the theology of religions provides a groundwork for further work in comparative theology. Comparative theology considers and reflects on other faith traditions with the express purpose of gaining new insight on the faith commitments of one's own tradition. This simple statement hides the complexity of the learning process. Comparative theology is an ongoing and never-ending learning project. But prior to such extended work, at a foundational level, Christian theology itself has to have built into it an openness to other faith traditions and some fundamental commitments that are instructive for appropriating the nature of the enterprise. Listening to and learning from other religious traditions factor into a Christian imagination dimensions that can be crucial for constructive Christian self-understanding in our pluralistic religious world. What follows illustrates this point.

---

[11] Edward Schillebeeckx, *Church: The Human Story of God* (New York: Crossroad, 1990), 165.

[12] Ibid., 166–67.

Learning Faith and Revelation from Judaism

Judaism illustrates the mediation of God through historical events. Abraham Joshua Heschel explains how Jewish faith rests upon historical experiences. The framework for understanding Judaism consists of momentous historical events at the foundation of this ancient people and how these root experiences hold them together. Remembering and celebrating these events make their relevance actual; the community is one because Jews all over the world simultaneously participate in these events through ritual and moral actions.[13] Emil Fackenheim highlights two such constitutive "root experiences" in the salvation at the Red Sea and the commanding divine presence at Sinai. These were historical experiences of public events, not otherworldly experiences; Jews escaped from Egypt and the law formalized their relation with God. What occurred before the eyes of the witnesses "was not an opening of heaven but a transformation of earth—an historic event affecting decisively all future Jewish generations."[14] These were natural historical events, but they revealed the presence of God.

Jewish faith exemplifies well the threefold structure of historical revelation. Alfred North Whitehead describes revealed religion in these terms: "[It] claims that its concepts, though derived primarily from special experiences, are yet of universal validity, to be applied by faith to the ordering of all experience."[15] All revelation is communication to human consciousness. It occurs in history and thus in a particular time. Yet the experience is such that it illumines all reality. By opening up human consciousness to ultimate reality, everything appears in a new light. A faith tradition consists of a community of people who remember the revelatory events, interpret them, keep them alive, and live into a promised future.

---

[13] Abraham Joshua Heschel, "The Moment at Sinai," in *Moral Grandeur and Spiritual Audacity*, ed. Susannah Heschel (New York: Farrar, Straus and Giroux, 1996), 12–17.

[14] Emil L. Fackenheim, *God's Presence in History: Jewish Affirmations and Philosophical Reflections* (New York: Harper Torchbooks, 1972), 10.

[15] Alfred North Whitehead, *Religion in the Making* (Cleveland: New York: Meridian Books, World Publishing, 1960), 31.

Jewish theology rejects a God who is not involved in history or is withdrawn from history. But God does not overwhelm history and allows room for freedom and for evil. Although God is portrayed in scripture anthropomorphically and as acting on behalf of Israel, God is not a finite actor within history. God uses agents to accomplish God's will. The God of Jewish faith is God and not an idol, a transcendent God who promises a future salvation that applies to each person and all history.[16]

Jewish theology closely ties God to the community as a chosen people, so that God and the Jewish community form a close, reciprocal, covenantal bond. The God of Sinai is sovereign and lawgiver. The law became the bond, the agreement, the contract that united God to this people and gave this people its identity as a community that is tied to God. But Judaism does not assume an exclusivist stance. One could say that Judaism has always been too small to have universalist aspirations in terms of numbers. Some Jews regard the covenant as a deep human structure, so that Christianity may be considered as Judaism for Gentiles.[17] This illustrates how a committed self-understanding of being bound to ultimate reality in a completely unique way can recognize that God may also be related to others in a different but analogously unique way. Such a faith is not divisive because it is not competitive; it reaches out to see something analogous to itself in other religious traditions. The "universality" of primal Jewish experiences consists of all Jews recognizing and participating in those common Jewish experiences at any given time. The events are revelations of God who through them established Jewish identity; the events symbolically constituted their permanent relationship with God. But they are relevant for others as well.

Judaism also has had to reckon with the tension created when the God of history does not appear to act in history. Jewish faith finds God mediated by history and as active in history; it also calls

---

[16] Fackenheim, *God's Presence in History*, 19.
[17] Michael S. Kogan, *Opening the Covenant: A Jewish Theology of Christianity* (Oxford: University Press, 2008), 33–35, 239–40.

for Jews to respond by being active in history according to God's law, which is never repressive but always favors human flourishing. But where was God during the Holocaust? This horrific human event, whose religious proportions cannot be measured, is not an exclusively Jewish issue; ultimately it is shared by all. Like a huge common human problem, it affects all religions as a question, all traditions of theology that are not immune to human suffering, and each one's particular faith. Where is God or ultimate reality in the immensity of the world's corporate degradation of human life, in innocent suffering, and in extreme forms of personal tragedy? Jewish theology has no easy answer and has to accept the mystery of life's "whirlwind." The idea that this is God's punishment, besides being depressingly anthropomorphic, makes no sense in terms of elemental justice. The God of Israel's history is the covenantal protector of God's beloved people, and that God appeared to be absent.

Fackenheim addresses the contemporary Jewish attachment to God after the Holocaust in a manner that is large in its scope, dramatic in its direct statement, and breathtaking in its courage. In contrast to all the impossible theological explanations, Fackenheim simply appeals to God's accompaniment. Wherever Israel has traveled or found itself, *Shekinah,* or God's presence, was with them. This profound conviction places God with Jews in their innocent suffering. In Fackenheim's words: "The Jew would be in exile, but not cut off from the divine Presence. He could still hold fast to history, for the God who had been present in history once was present in it still and would in the end bring total redemption."[18]

This need not be a private Jewish experience or sentiment. It increasingly seems to be summoned forth from all theist religions. But Christianity in particular has inherited its basic character, and it appears at several junctures. Christianity is mediated by the historical event of Jesus of Nazareth; the mediation effected liberation; the community carries forward the authority of God and God's law; it subsists in the same covenant relationship and draws forth a moral response from the community that engages history.

---

[18] Fackenheim, *God's Presence in History*, 29.

Appreciating the Bond with Islam

Islam seems distant from Christianity, yet Muslims make up the largest faith tradition in North America after Christianity. Islam seems totally different from Christianity, and yet it shares Jewish and Christian revelations, and both are represented in the Qur'an. Christianity and Islam are both sprawling traditions with multiple axes of internal divisions and contextual sociopolitical incarnations, yet both are united in monotheism and a covenant with the same Abrahamic God. Christianity, in passing through Greece, became deeply concerned with doctrine; Islam stressed submission to God in prayer and following God's will. Across a gulf that has been called a clash of civilizations, Western Christians have to work at finding the deeper bonds that connect us with Islam and what can be learned from it.

Islamic faith is based on the Qur'an, God's self-revelation to the final messenger after Moses and Jesus. The Qur'an consists of God's words, spoken to Muhammad, in Arabic. After Muhammad's death in sixth-century Arabia, the movement spread in a divided leadership of Sunnis and Shiites. Today Muslims are spread around the world but are united by the Qur'an in a foundational belief in God and a final day of judgment. They share common practices of prayer five times a day, fasting, contribution to social care of the poor, and pilgrimage to Mecca, the birthplace of Muhammad and Islam itself. The Qur'an gives Islam a close relationship with Middle Eastern culture. But three areas related to doctrine open up themes that can deepen Christian theology: the character of God, isolating the core of faith; and finding the ground for religious pluralism in the face of self-conscious particularism and exclusivism.

On an abstract level the conception of God in Islam appears to resemble God in Judaism and Christianity. The name of God is Allah, which means "the God." "Without doubt the Qur'an's most insistent assertion is that God is one, to the exclusion of all others, and this has become the heart of the Muslim profession of faith."[19]

---

[19] Daniel A. Madigan, "Themes and Topics," in *The Cambridge Companion to the Qur'an*, ed. Jane Dammen McAuliffe (Cambridge: Cambridge University Press, 2007), 80. Madigan canvasses the Qur'an and constructs an abstract

God is sovereign creator, and one can read the character of God in the created world of nature; the whole of creation shows that God has designed creation for human existence. The human response of faith, then, is first of all total submission to the will of God, and this has to be mixed with gratitude. The abiding connection between faith and gratitude for God creating us shows that one without faith is a *kafir*, an ingrate.

God minutely attends to human life. God sends messengers in angels and prophets to point people to the signs of God all around them, to call people to faith, to remind people of God's blessings, and to warn of the consequences of infidelity. God also keeps accounts. God keeps the record of human deeds for judgment after death. God balances justice and mercy. "Earthly creation is seen as a testing ground for humanity: 'God made the heavens and the earth in truth, so that each soul could be rewarded for what is earned.'"[20] Abstractly, the God of Islam is the God of Jews and Christians, but the themes of complete submission to God—in prayer, confession of faith, and attention to God's will—give Allah a distinctive place in Muslim life.

This may be illustrated by a 2007 document addressed to Pope Benedict XVI responding to a public statement of his that characterized Muslim faith negatively. It insists on the closeness of the inner core of Muslim and Christian faith framed in terms of love of God and love of neighbor. The peace and understanding between Muslims and Christians are founded on these grounds in both faiths:

> Love of the One God, and love of the neighbor. These principles
> are found over and over again in the sacred texts of Islam and
> Christianity. The Unity of God, the necessity of love for Him,

---

synthetic description of the idea or notion of God in Islam. But the concept of God is transformed by the practices of prayer and the disposition of Muslim life.

[20] Ibid., 90, citing Qur'an, 45:22. "In the final analysis, the Qur'an is concerned to assert God's tendency to forgive rather than to condemn." It consistently asserts that God is forgiving, generous, merciful, and loving. This is the basic motive for sending messengers (Madigan, "Themes and Topics," 91).

and the necessity of love of the neighbor is thus the common ground between Islam and Christianity.[21]

The letter concludes: "It is clear that the *Two Greatest Commandments* are an area of common ground and a link between the Qur'an, the Torah and the New Testament."[22]

At the same time, Islam also shares with Christianity internal divisions. The student of Islam has to marvel how this single identifiable faith tradition has taken many different turns in its expanding world context. Like someone approaching Christianity from the outside finds a dizzying number of traditions, churches, denominations, and congregations that have histories of hostility toward one another, so too Islam takes many different forms, and each has a historical explanation. Study of the analogies are informative in both directions.

Islam displays another tension that has a parallel in Christianity, so analysis here is instructive. The Qur'an balances an openness to other religious traditions, especially Judaism and Christianity, with a need of the Muslim community for its own identity. Two dimensions of its relation to God pull against each other: one recognizes the unity of all human beings in relation to the creator God; the other attends to the distinctiveness of God's revelation to Muhammad and the need for a unique identity of the community that represents that faith.[23] On the one hand, personal faith recognizes that the God of all, manifest in creation and present to all, forms a basis for all people having what is needed for final salvation. On the other hand, social coexistence with other religions pushes a community toward a sense of superiority and exclusivity. Two distinct theologies developed, one open to other Abrahamic

---

[21] *A Common Word between Us and You*, an open letter and call from Muslim religious leaders to Pope Benedict XVI and other Christian leaders, signed by a host of Muslim representatives, in October 2007. The text cited is from the summary statement that accompanied the letter.

[22] *A Common Word between Us and You*, Part III. Note the dialectics here: Before one tradition can learn from the differences of the other, there has to be a foundational openness to the other accompanied by mutual respect.

[23] Abdulaziz Sachedina, "The Qur'an and Other Religions," in McAuliffe, *The Cambridge Companion to the Qur'an*, 293.

traditions offering salvation, and the other, not fully validated by the Qur'an, a supersessionist theology: no salvation outside the revelation to the prophet Muhammad.[24]

The result was two distinct lines of interpretation in the Muslim world: one open to humans as responsible for their destiny, with an ability to read the presence of God in creation, and an appreciation of the efficacy of other monotheistic revelations to support a saving faith; the other holding Islam as the absolute or exclusive religious tradition. The first finds support in personal attachment to God the sovereign creator; the second is stimulated by a context of rivalry and competition. The comparison of this tension in both Islam and Christianity shows that each faith tradition can learn more about itself by studying the other.

Learning from Buddhist Difference

Many Christians are attracted to Buddhist practices of meditation. The quest for mindfulness bores deeply into self-consciousness and opens up the surrounding world to new light. But Buddhism also consists of a larger way of life and a complex worldview that not only differs from but at certain points seems to contradict Christian belief. Where Christians and Buddhists share the same beliefs, neither has anything dramatic to learn from the other. By contrast, appropriating something that seems quite different into Christian self-understanding requires explanation of how it can authentically both be Buddhist and become Christian.

Two theoretical considerations drawn from the work of Perry Schmidt-Leukel explain how a theist religion can learn from Buddhist non-theism about the relationship between human beings and God. The first principle states that religious traditions are comparable, that the differences among religions can also be found within each religion. One can find common patterns across religious traditions, and also within each one. And these differences find echoes in the

---

[24] Beneath the rise of exclusivism lurks a need for "self-identification and self-defense of a group against other absolute truth claims" (ibid., 298).

orientations of individual persons.[25] This means that religious traditions, rooted in very different historical contexts, remain comparable.
The second, more practical, principle is that one can fully respect
the differences between traditions and, at the same time, find functional analogies between elements within each one.[26] This means
that the concepts drawn from one tradition are not identical with that
to which they are compared, but they play an analogous function.
One can say of Gautama, Jesus, and Muhammad that each one in a
unique way was awakened, proclaimed his message to others, and
embodied ultimate reality.[27] In sum, within one's own religion one
can find patterns that are comparable to ones found in radically different faith traditions, and it is possible to appropriate the concepts
from another radically different tradition by a functional rather than
a conceptual analogy.

Using these principles two Buddhist ideas may deepen analogous
thinking in Christian theology. In the first case, the idea of non-duality
helps Christians appreciate more accurately the relationship between
God and the world. The second notes how the Buddhist idea of non-
self or no-self might influence Christian cosmology and anthropology.

First, a premise in Buddhism that Christians can identify with
has roots in the experience of time: all things are in process and
nothing lasts. The *Dhammapada* describes the relentless repetition of
time: it creates and it destroys. As such, time defines the structure of
existence and personal life. "I have wandered on and on, searching

---

[25] Perry Schmidt-Leukel, "A Fractal Interpretation of Religious Diversity: An
Overview," in *New Paths for Interreligious Theology: Perry Schmidt-Leukel's
Fractal Interpretation of Religious Diversity*, ed. Alan Race and Paul Knitter
(Maryknoll, NY: Orbis Books, 2019), 3.

[26] As Schmidt-Leukel says of diverse concepts: "The connotations they carry
within their respective systems and their historical genealogies are simply too
different. But despite those undeniable differences they can be seen as 'functional equivalents'" (Perry Schmidt-Leukel, "Buddha and Christ as Mediators
of the Transcendent: A Christian Perspective," in *Buddhism and Christianity
in Dialogue: The Gerald Weisfeld Lectures 2004*, ed. Perry Schmidt-Leukel
[Norwich, Norfolk: SCM Press, 2005], 170).

[27] Schmidt-Leukel, *New Paths for Interreligious Theology*, 21. The parallels
among the three revealers correspond with the theory of revelation underlying
this book.

for, but never finding, the builder of this house. To be born again and again is suffering."[28] This personal experience mirrors reality: everything is part of a vast universe in constant motion. The Buddhist cosmology of "conditioned genesis" depicts each individual thing as temporarily participating in a massive wholeness, like froth on a wave in an ocean. In this constant cosmogenesis everything comes from something else for a time before passing into otherness. Thich Nhat Hanh uses the term *interbeing* to refer to the interconnection of all things, for the intertwined causal relationship between all things. Being mindful of God's presence for a Christian would be "very close to the Buddhist appreciation of interbeing and interpenetration."[29] Non-duality refers to an inseparable unity of distinct realities, the internal and reciprocal bond holding real differences together.

A Christian experience and a conception of the self and the world could be kept intact and yet truly altered by this conception. The doctrinal tradition, with its emphasis on what we can affirm, tends to objectify transcendence and place it over against us as object grasped by knowing subject. This structure tends toward a dualism that separates the ground of being from the subjects that experience it, entertain it, contemplate it, and relate to it.[30] Christianity insists against pantheism that the world is not God; God is other, and the world in itself is real. But the non-separability and interpenetration of God and the world, something the Christian mystical tradition so appreciates, tends to get lost in ordinary language. Christianity needs a doctrine of creation that coheres with scientific emergence and evolution and preserves the non-dual unity of God with the world-in-process and each individual within it. The earlier discussion of God's transcendence and immanence encourages this.

Second, a common antithesis between Christianity and Buddhism states that the Christian conception of God ratifies the identity and

---

[28] *The Dhammapada*, trans. Gil Fronsdal (Boston: Shambhala, 2006), #153. "All created things are impermanent" (#277).

[29] Thich Nhat Hanh, *Living Buddha, Living Christ* (New York: Riverhead Books, 1995), 28.

[30] Wendy Farley, "Duality and Non-Duality in Christian Practice: Reflections on the Benefits of Buddhist-Christian Dialogue for Constructive Theology," *Buddhist-Christian Studies* 31 (2011): 139.

work of the individual as plainly as Buddhism denies substantial selfhood. Again, the *Dhammapada* states it plainly: "All things are not-self." They have no substantial identity. "Seeing this with insight, one becomes disenchanted with suffering. This is the path to purity."[31] The *Kaccayanagotta Sutta* contrasts existence and nonexistence. Existence is so filled with suffering and stress that nonexistence is positive because suffering and stress are overcome. Everything that exists is either attachments and clinging or the overcoming and passing away of this preoccupation with the self.[32]

Moral interpretation of self-denial makes perfect sense across these faith traditions. But a moral reduction of "no-self" would lose something essential in Buddhism and its contribution to Christian self-understanding. The attempt to build up the self by clinging to other beings misunderstands the complete dependence of reality on its interconnectedness within the power of Dharma. Each individual being is part of the interconnected power of being, and it fills the self with being-as-process. "No-self" in the end is not denial and not negative; it is dialectical, a freedom that finds pure being within the self that is distinct from other things that the self only appears to need. This full freedom lies within the self; it is ultimately distinct from the phenomenal self and identical with it. Christianity will benefit from a doctrine of creation that preserves the autonomy of the individual precisely in the dependence of being created.

Understanding and Dealing with Religious Pluralism

This chapter has covered much ground; it needs a summary and a conclusion. It intends a formal or structural response to the challenge

---

[31] *Dhammapada*, #279.

[32] Some interpret this as a moral and not a metaphysical doctrine. This is suggested by verses of the *Dhammapada*: "Destroy attachment to self as you could an autumn lily in your fist. Cultivate the path to peace, the Nirvana taught by the Well-Gone-One" (#285); "The destruction of craving conquers all suffering" (#354). Combine these verses with those that insist on self-responsibility (One is one's own protector; there is no outside help) and one can conclude that self and no-self are moral categories that presuppose a moral agent or subject.

that relativism poses to all religion and to theology as a critical discipline. The response to relativism lies in religious pluralism, but it
too seems to disturb religious commitment. This chapter, therefore,
argues that religious pluralism represents a natural and a positive
feature of religious consciousness. Interreligious dialogue is both
the witness and the proof of that assertion. Taken together, these
features underline several qualities of the discipline of theology. Its
authentic source and inspiration remain transcendent; all religious
consciousness is historically conditioned and therefore limited, but
theological affirmation retains the symbolic realism established in
the previous chapter. Theologies can thus learn from one another.

It should be clear that relativism is a spontaneous but ultimately
hasty and ignorant response to reality. So many things of a metaphysical kind that can be said about the nature of reality, culled from
diverse humanistic and scientific disciplines, enable cross-cultural
communication about the common human situation. Although transcendent ultimate reality does not lie exposed to a common vision,
ultimate concern is a common human response; it suggests the
existence of and encourages a quest for transcendent reality. The
logical retort to relativism, that it expresses an ultimate metaphysical
worldview, transcends mere verbal assertion and describes how all
people live by some faith. The real problem lies in historicity: no
one can grasp the absolute absolutely.

Theologians also have to give some rationale for why religious
pluralism may be considered a positive situation. That constructive
response has to begin with a description of the way things are. The
hard sciences ratify an expanded human experience that reality
consists of a constant interrelated flow of data and uninterrupted
becoming. Within the shell of nature's patterns of behavior, time bears
constant witness to diverse particular beings interacting to produce
novelty. Common structures of human perception and understanding exist within a world of motion and the interaction of particular
beings. Held against a fictional background of universal sameness,
the flow of being and process thinking offer vitality, novelty, and
new knowledge of new being. Reality is a narrative, not just in the
telling, but in its relentless motion. This does not negate universal
patterns of thought any more than do random occurrence and novelty

curtail the laws of nature. But thinking, to correspond with reality, has to keep up with time.

Religious consciousness, and derivatively theology, cannot be lifted out of the natural human condition. There can be clear transcendental or universal guidelines for the nature of religious consciousness, but however religious experience is defined, it will always exist in unique and particular ways. The source of Christian theology is the transcendent God, but as revealed principally in Jesus of Nazareth and always received within a particular historical context. The basic formula, then, runs like this: transcendence within finitude; the unconditioned in particular experience; single God or ultimate reality in so many different forms of actual consciousness. The limitations of human consciousness translate into limitations upon theological affirmation, but not its realism. One can know something with certainty and at the same time know there is more to be known.

These convictions open up for theology a world of interfaith dialogue and conversation. Wilfred Cantwell Smith wrote passionately about a world theology that may have impressed some to think wrongly that one could overcome particularity by producing a single theology with many faith traditions as its informants.[33] Pluralism is unity in difference. There can never be a single theology. But there can be a human family talking theology with one another. This does not prevent theological affirmation from being realistic and true; it only encourages it to be humble, inquiring, and respectful of other faith traditions.

---

[33] Wilfred Cantwell Smith, *Towards a World Theology: Faith and the Comparative History of Religion* (London: Macmillan, 1981).

4

Theology in the Face of Evil

The temptation of cosmic pessimism was described in Chapter 1. The phrase suggests a new version of the question that evil poses to theism. This reaction corresponds to more than personal tragedy and even episodic disaster and correlates with something more abiding and discouraging. Global news communicates an all-enveloping shroud of negativity that wears people down and drains a sense of ultimate hope from worldly existence. The unrelenting cycle of life and death reduces flourishing and fulfillment to an immediate personal goal. Reaching beyond that seems like wishful thinking. What are the contours of this situation, and how does it affect the dynamics of theology?

There is little doubt that the amount of evil in the world makes belief in God the creator more difficult. Sometimes, when some personal tragedy strikes the self or someone close, people suddenly find themselves standing before the void. And the global statistics of human degradation and innocent suffering are too great to reduce pessimism to a personal experience of suffering and loss of meaning. The amount of sheer deprivation, of poverty, hunger, focused human hatred, and vast lack of opportunity for natural human development, casts a pall over human existence itself. An ultimate pessimism often rests on cumulative reasons that are actual; it is supported by evidence. It therefore requires reflection; theology cannot simply go forward without responding. In many ways the temptation to pessimism sets the bar for theology's credibility. Theology cannot be escapist.

Science has introduced a new framework for understanding humanity. The discovery of the temporal emergence of the universe, the recognition of the evolution of life, and the continuing social evolution of the human species force a narrative understanding of human existence. The character of the human, human nature, manifests itself most accurately as a result of process, a product of time. Human nature gradually broke out of mechanism into higher forms of consciousness and freedom. The knowing capacity of human beings and their creativity now seem to grow exponentially. We are evolving socially into an actual single community of interacting persons, groups, and nations. But this stunning story of evolution has cost a price of suffering that leaves the imagination limp.

Science throws a less hopeful light on the quality of life for masses of individuals. Surely human intelligence has refashioned human existence with wonderful new powers through ingenious technological creativity. But the human species also reflects in its own way the conflictive, competitive character of natural selection. Human beings compete as fiercely and mortally with each other as they do with other species who get in their way. The history of human lives together testifies as much to mutual destruction as it does to the mutual enhancement of life. History yields only fragments of a positive interpretation of human lives together in harmony.[1] If we are to speak of a God of love, whose cause is for human fulfillment, we need a constructive heuristic framework in order to receive the revelation of a positive future. Adjusting the understanding of the nature of theology, its point of departure, its method, and its expectations, can help clarify the sources of hope.

A theological response to the temptation of pessimism moves through stages. It begins with revelation as simultaneously a disclosure about humankind. Human existence appears in a new way in the light of an encounter with ultimate reality. Christian revelation of God also opens up an awareness of sinful potential, that is, a consciousness that human existence itself bears a negative aggressiveness within itself. The recognition that human existence

---

[1] These fragments, however, are real; they play an important role in constructive understanding. More is said on fragments further on.

contains within itself sources of the great negativities of history is a first step in a theological response to pessimism.

A second step turns to the discipline of theology itself. Theology up to this point has appeared to be an exercise in intellectual reflection. But the condition of human existence as extensively crushed by evil and marked by sin turns theology into a practical discipline. Practical in this case means recognizing and guiding people through negative human situations that restrict human development, turn it back on itself, and leave people passive, discouraged, and diminished. In response to the negative dimensions of human existence, theology appears as an interpretive discipline, one that converts the Christian message into a way of life that is meant to foster human freedom and a life that leads to flourishing and fulfillment. A practical discipline will thus encourage a positive and constructive way of life. The positive potential of a Christian view of life is analyzed here against pessimism; the contents of Christian life itself will be addressed in Chapter 7.

As a practical discipline, thirdly, theology also has an intrinsic ethical dimension. Whether or not its ethical drift is made explicit, theological understanding always responds to some human interest. A consideration of the method of the discipline shows how Christian theology is oriented toward justice (and against injustice) and toward building up the common good against the institutionalized obstacles to human development that are recognized as destructive.

A fourth step consists of illustrating the practical logic of theology in the work of two distinct theologians who exemplify it. James Cone and Gustavo Gutiérrez represent in analogous ways and on a formal level an alternative to pessimism. Their liberation theologies show that the response to sin has to be more than repentance; it has to assume some form of action that resists the dimensions of sin that structure public and private lives. These two theologians, along with many others, illustrate not "identity" theologies but the inherent liberating structure of Christian theology.

The key to this discussion of theology as a practical humanistic discipline rests on the insight that the negativities that plague human existence also offer a conscious entrée into a positive world of liberation. This sphere includes but transcends personal liberation;

it carries an impulse to strive for social freedom. Christian theology proposes a positive humanism because it is a message of social justice and liberation.

Revelation of Human Existence before God

Revelation of ultimate reality always involves revelation of human existence. The transcendent object of revelation cannot be compared with the finite objects of everyday reckoning. Encountering transcendence simultaneously draws human attention to the transcendent object. Human consciousness, therefore, cannot divorce an awareness of the presence of God from a consciousness of itself standing before God. Anyone who encounters God, or more generally transcendent reality, becomes implicated in what is encountered. Christian revelation reveals human existence standing before the face of God.

Revelation should not be conceived of as a verbal message from God to a listener. Anthropomorphic language seriously misleads at this point. The previous chapters altered the conception of revelation as object-to-subject transmission of information by means of the idea of non-duality. Revelation makes more sense as disclosure of the ultimate within the self. The images of "light" and "horizon" provide better metaphors for how revelation expands the human field of vision. By mediating a presence of God to and within human existence, revelation sheds light on the human as we know it and expands the perspective on the things we continue to learn about the human phenomenon.

The idea of sin is not essential or intrinsic to human existence as such. But the biblical story of primeval existence symbolizes an inner drive for existence that will grasp at anything that appears to enhance the self. An evolutionary world suggests some primal desire to live that confronts all obstacles to survival. What Buddhists call grasping and clinging, Christians call temptation and the wellspring of sin. The term *sin* is used here in a simple way to refer to the evil that in some degree has its source in human freedom and exercises its energy through human choices. Sin in this sense is distinct from natural evil, events that destroy life devoid of conscious intent, simply as part of the mechanisms of nature. Sin, by contrast, has roots in the many varying degrees of personal freedom. Although a function of freedom, it appears intractable because of the natural, personal, and social tendencies that stimulate what appears to be reflective and deliberate action. Theology, inspired by revelation, and mediated through faith, has to deal with human existence and cannot avoid the phenomenon of sin.

The biblical story of Adam and Eve represents pristine human existence, in contrast to a perfect creation, as disobedient and re-bellious, not from the hands of the creator, but moved by an ambi-tious and aggressive spirit. The Book of Genesis shows that God fashions human existence out of the earth. When the narratives are fitted into an evolutionary context, they tell how freedom itself lies behind much of human suffering and oppression. Paul Ricoeur has described how the early symbolism of evil places its roots within a competitive human striving that always wants to live more ful-ly.[2] Each person experiences an inner drive to want more and to get more, sometimes at the expense of others. Whether this energy comes to reflective self-awareness or not, it represents a dimension of biological life that has become conscious.

When a competitive spirit operates socially, it loses many of the personal control mechanisms of an individual conscience. Social life is a strange mixture of freedom and spontaneous or habitual response. Social competition betrays an attenuated reflective and moral freedom; social groups rarely serve others against their own interests. It has become relatively easy for theologians today to translate what the tradition called original sin into a "sin of the world." The many ingrained social relationships that institutionalize social life at its various levels contain social hostilities that support aggressive behavior against others. The idea of a "social sin" contains an immense abstraction summarizing the way social institutions, in seeking their own goals, lessen the personal responsibility of their constituents. In attending to their own positive goals, either inten-tionally or inadvertently, people frequently damage other people's lives. The very dynamics of social life, set within the context of

---

[2] Paul Ricoeur, *The Symbolism of Evil* (Boston: Beacon Press, 1969), 232–60.

the struggle of everyone for survival and gain, make sin seem indigenous to human life. In sum, Christian revelation includes an implicit anthropology. Although temptation, in the form of a drive to survive, is part of human existence, formal sin is not essential to human nature, and human beings are called by God to resist it at every level.[3]

Theology as a Humanistic Discipline

In order to show how Christian theology positively responds to the flawed sinful character of actual human existence, one has to be clear about the logic of theology itself. Discussions of the nature of theology entail endless intricate questions about the critical method of the discipline. This discussion sidesteps these details and fixes attention on how theology is a theoretical academic study that has practical humanistic application. With this in mind, the discussion turns to a theory of interpretation in order to arrive at a definition of theology as interpretation of the world through the symbols of Christian faith. That analysis of theology as a field of learning sets up the consideration of how theology contains within itself a foundation for ethical responses to life in the present world.

One can begin with the principle that to know is to interpret. Interpretation is not a human operation that is added on to knowing; rather, all knowing, at every level, is always at the same time interpreting. Perception, experience, recognition of meaning, insight into structure or value, understanding something or some operation, judgment about the truth of a theory, or the consensus of a group, all involve interpretation that will vary with human knowers. As was established earlier, human consciousness is inescapably perspectival.

Theology on the face of it consists of interpretation of the Christian faith as it is contained in its sources. This describes in a self-evident

---

[3] This section on a recognition of sin in standing before God cannot be counted as an adequate theology of sin. Sin refers to something as profound as human existence itself, which cannot be considered "in passing." But neither can this topic be ignored. What is said here can only serve as a topic for discussion.

way what theologians do, prior to a careful analysis of what is going on in the process of interpretation itself. Several discrete factors enter into theological interpretation. How theologians put these variables together differs greatly across periods of history, cultures, schools of theology, and individual theologians. Other disparities come into play at any given time: particular perspectives based on race, ethnic identity, position in society, and loyalties to a particular political viewpoint. A deep concern for particularity today has multiplied the number of the variables in interpretation almost by the number of the interpreters. There may be a structural commonality across patterns of knowing and interpretation, but, because of history and social perspective, the same methods of interpretation may yield different conclusions.

Moving back to a broad matrix for understanding theology as interpretation of the faith of the community, it is generally agreed that theologians have at their disposal the common sources that represent the faith of the community in objective or public forms. The primary Christian source for theology is the Bible, the New and Old Testaments that make up scripture. These writings provide the most direct and agreed upon sources of theology across different Christian traditions, denominations, and churches. Scripture is the house of Christian revelation, not revelation itself, which exists in human consciousness, but its earliest, most direct, public, and ac-cepted representation. There are other fonts for theological reflec-tion: the traditions of creeds, doctrines, church confessions, stable traditions that span churches, and theological figures who help define a common but pluralistic linguistic tradition. These many sources find their roots in scripture. Although tradition offers other sources for theology, as a conception it includes scripture within itself. Thus, one could use the shorthand formula that theology consists in interpreting scripture or interpreting Christian tradition.

The consensus that Christian theology consists in interpreting scripture elicits attention to the process of the interpretation itself. What does interpretation mean? Is there a common or universal method of interpretation? Often interpretation seems to be as diverse as the variables just enumerated. Although these questions open up endless debates, it is possible to make some generalizations that may be accepted by most and still provide some traction for determining some basic components common to all theological interpretation. A model for such an understanding may be drawn from mutual human communication and intersubjective understanding. More particularly, the metaphor for the method of theology employed here is conversation.[4] The way two people come to understand each other is conversation. Mutual communication, interpretation, and conversation amount to the same process. It essentially consists in the back and forth of speaking and listening, listening and replying, and listening again.

The metaphor of a conversation contains some noteworthy elements. One is that communication and mutual understanding do not happen all at once. They require an extended process, because human subjects are deep and their individuality normally cannot be summed up in a word. This makes intersubjective communication an appropriate framework for understanding the subject matter of theology because both the human person and the ultimate share a mystery that cannot be laid out objectively.[5] And yet, there is enough shared in common between human subjects that communication is possible. If two persons with utterly different cultures and languages meet and wish to communicate, they will create a language that bridges them. This points to a second idea about the way communication works. People can communicate basic human experiences across all historical boundaries by analogy. One can usually resonate with basic human experiences, feelings, and understandings of other unique individuals because one finds analogous experiences within the self.[6] This structure constitutes the basic bridge by which the interpreter of scripture can read the linguistic signs of past revelatory

---

[4] David Tracy, "Theological Interpretation of the Scriptures in the Church: Prospect and Retrospect," in Robert M. Grant, *A Short History of the Interpretation of the Bible* (Minneapolis: Fortress Press, 1984), 181.

[5] See Kathryn Tanner, "In the Image of the Invisible," in *Apophatic Bodies: Negative Theology, Incarnation, and Relationality*, ed. Chris Boesel and Catherine Keller (New York: Fordham University Press Online, 2011), 117–34.

[6] David Tracy, *The Analogical Imagination: Christian Theology and the Culture of Pluralism* (New York: Crossroad, 1981), 454–55.

language and find some analogous meaning within themselves and thus, more generally, for people who share the interpreter's world.

Interpretation conceived as a conversation, or in simpler terms as a dialogue between the text and the interpreter, moves in two directions. The interpreter reads and construes the text, and the text sends a message to the one reading it. On the one hand, the sources of Christian theology bear a message and the interpreters actively seek its meaning through implicit questions. On the other hand, the text actively communicates with those ready to receive the message.[7] Each side is active and passive at the same time. All of this is always going on simultaneously in the process of dialogue with the sources of Christian revelation. The exchange offers a fairly accurate description of the discipline of Christian theology across time and cultures. But the simplicity of the description does not approach the complexity of the process, whether in personal interpretation or community appropriation. In fact, corporate theological reflection always involves a conflict of interpretations due to the individuality of the theologian, the primary community, and the many variables in the process. Theology involves a conversation of many partners and not a simple one-on-one exchange with the sources of a community's faith.

The twofold direction involved in the structure of dialogue helps to account for two major types or classes of theology. The first type of theology stresses the movement from the text to the interpreter. It lays an emphasis on what the sources of revelation have to say to the present moment. In many situations one can presuppose an audience for theology that already accepts and by and large understands the meaning of the Christian symbols that hold the community together. More important, the individuals in that audience accept the authority of the sources. But they may not understand fully or more pointedly how these symbols apply to the exigencies of the present moment. For example, this chapter considers how the Christian message ad-

---

[7] This schematic phrasing does not imply an authorless text. A text is a window on a world of meaning. Nor should the example of a text be understood reductively; other symbols provide media for interpreting the meaning of Christian revelation.

dresses the prevalence of sin in the world, how it can undermine the grounds for comprehensive meaning and value. This type of theology moves from the symbols of faith to their application in the present situation. It is often didactic and declarative and frequently called kerygmatic or evangelical in the sense of the rootedness of its language in the gospel. The focus of its critical questioning falls more decidedly on application of Christian symbols to life than on the intrinsic meaningfulness of the symbols.

The second type stresses the movement from the theologian to the text; it places emphasis on a search for the meaning of the sources of a Christian tradition, principally scripture, that lack traction because of their distance from the present. Because of the cultural gap, traditional witness requires formal attention to the process by which the interpreter retrieves meaning for the different and non-comprehending present. Familiar language to which a community is accustomed may be sending messages that differ greatly from the original intent on basic matters. Much of theology consists in applying the principles of interpretation in order to make the sources of revelation comprehensible to a present-day culture. For example, much of Chapter 2 discussed the basic meaning of faith and revelation to a culture that is conditioned to be suspicious of the claims of religion. Depending on the audience, the fundamental weight of a theology may fall on explaining the traditional meaning of the public symbols that represent the content of the faith community in terms that make sense today. This type of theology is frequently called apologetic; it does not presuppose an appropriate understanding of the symbols of faith but seeks to render them intelligible in the terms of the culture being addressed.

These two dimensions are always in play in the back and forth of a conversation, so that neither of these broad types excludes the other. At the same time, the two directions often point to different audiences, and this influences the point of departure of a discussion, the underlying quality or theme of the reasoning, and the questions that are addressed. This gets more complicated when theology seeks to address pluralistic audiences. Frequently these foci and intentionalities are mixed in a given theology. The two large types, therefore, correspond to emphases, and the dividing lines and proportionalities of weight are not governed by a fixed formula. Awareness of these accents in theology help in the understanding of what is going on in any given theology. Chapter 2 of this book reflects an interpretation of the meaning of Christian symbols on the basis of critical reflection on knowing. The present chapter represents interpreting the world of evil and sin through the symbols of Christian faith.

This wide discussion of method and types of theology helps to formulate a way of defining theology as a practical humanistic academic discipline. Many instinctively turn to the components of the word *theology* to explain the subject matter of the discipline. But the etymological definition, "reflection on God," does little to describe the actual academic discipline. The scope of theology clearly reaches beyond a preoccupation with God as subject matter. Another common designation, "faith seeking understanding," appears to provide a base for more sophisticated explanations of the mechanics of the subject matter and method from various religious points of view. The definition is descriptive of much theology, but it narrows the field of vision to the boundaries of the given community and does not account for the way the biases of secular culture also exist inside the church. The conversation partners have expanded to include world, culture, science, and other religions.

A clarifying twist on a conception of the discipline of theology comes from the paradoxical claim of a Buddhist to be doing theology. Rita Gross does not describe her theology as talk about God, and she explicitly directs her writing toward a public audience. "As a Buddhist scholar-theologian, my agenda is to bring my experiential knowledge of Buddhist thought and practice into discussions of contemporary issues and problems, to work with the collective wisdom, compassion, and skillfulness of Buddhist traditions to suggest ways of alleviating the individual and collective suffering rampant in the world."[8] There is no reason, she adds, why this should not have a place in the academy. Analogously, Christian theology casts its eyes over the whole of reality from

---

[8] Rita M. Gross, "Buddhist Theology?" in *Buddhist Theology: Critical Reflections by Contemporary Buddhist Scholars,* ed. Roger Jackson and John Makransky (London: Routledge, 2000), 55.

the perspective of the particular religious symbols of the community.[9] Theology discusses the world in which we live; its specific sources include the public symbols of the faith tradition of the practitioners but shares other public resources as well. Christian theology is critical interpretation of the world through the symbols of the Christian community.

Theology and Ethics

Reflection on the relation of theology to ethics is needed to solidify the practical relation of theology to culture, especially to those aspects of society that contribute to cosmic pessimism. The previous section established that theology consists of interpretation and application of Christian symbols to understanding the world and the place of humans in it. The meaningfulness of theological terms requires some correlation with ordinary human experience critically considered. That correlation ensures that the conclusions of theological construction have some bearing on both understanding and living everyday human life. What remains is the question of how theology responds to cosmic pessimism. That will be found in the connection that weds Christian theological understanding with the ethical principles that are implied in and govern human life together.

The point here is not to provide anything like a system or a developed set of basic principles. The topic really focuses on an ethical imagination, a place where the consideration of the rightness and the goodness of human behavior are lodged. A bond between theology and ethics means that theology bears an intrinsic relationship to the character of corporate life in the world. The discussion offers a theory of the foundations of ethical experience that directly counters cosmic pessimism. It then shows that ethics is not an add-on to an established theology but an intrinsic concern of the theological imagination from the beginning.

---

[9] See also Thomas Aquinas, *Summa Theologiae*, I, 1, 7. The object of theology is the world; the sources of theology are the symbols of revelation.

A descriptive account of the roots of ethics may be found in what Edward Schillebeeckx called a negative experience of contrast.[10] Patricia McAuliffe shows how these negative experiences provide a basis for ethics and a platform for the meaningfulness of theology for social life. The place to begin this discussion is a description of a negative experience of contrast, which has an elementary structure of three dimensions.

First, it is an intuitive or "direct" rather than inferred experience that something, some situation or activity, is wrong, or negative. Something that exists is spontaneously perceived as something that should not be!

But, second, it could only be so appreciated against the background of at least an implicit recognition of the way things should be, of positivity. Otherwise one would not be able to recognize negativity as such. "In order even to recognize hunger, torture, and racism as negative, as what should not and cannot go on, we must experience them as in contrast with something else, something which is positive and good."[11] On the level of intelligibility, the same dialectic or contrast appears between meaninglessness and meaning. If something appears unintelligible, it is because one has an implicit formal grasp, whether clear or fuzzy, of what would constitute coherence.

A third element in this dialectical tension is ethical and moral in character: an implicit urge to right the wrong, correct the mistake, resist or negate the negativity. This common element of resistance to negativity is less a clear knowledge and more a practice, an active desire to do something to resolve the tension, to turn the negative into something positive.

These experiences are not rare; they are universal, because suffering and death are universal. They can be small, as in something interfering with a smooth personal relationship, or massive, like

---

[10] Schillebeeckx borrowed this analysis from critical social theory but nowhere developed it at great length. This representation of Schillebeeckx's understanding and use of the category is drawn from Patricia McAuliffe, "The Negative Contrast Experience Is Foundational for Ethics," in *Fundamental Ethics: A Liberationist Approach* (Washington, DC: Georgetown University Press, 1993), 1–38.

[11] Ibid., 6.

witnessing the destruction of our habitat. They are an intrinsic part of human existence, and they supply the experiential grid or field in which the very ideas of salvation and liberation originate, that is, by contrast with existing situations.

Much of traditional ethics and theology begin abstractly with universal principles and norms of an ideal world. They begin on the supposition of the order of nature or harmony in the universe and build on "what is positive, abstract, and universal in the world or in human nature."[12] By contrast, negative experiences give rise to liberation theologies and liberation ethics. These disciplines have their deep roots in negativity; they begin their reflection with experience of a fragmented disorderly world rather than a deceptive conception of harmony. Liberationist thinking reckons with a human nature that is damaged and marked by brokenness, suffering, and need.[13]

McAuliffe's point, echoing Schillebeeckx, is that the negativity that lies at the foundations of theology and ethics does not consist of a logical principle but of an experience. The negative experience of suffering provides the deep structure out of which theology and ethics arise. Christian theology reflects a quest for some form of salvation, and gradually the symbol of liberation is becoming the term that translates salvation for the modern period.[14] Theology follows human consciousness in seeking liberation in reaction against some form of suffering, or oppression, or negativity that, by constricting or suppressing human freedom, dehumanizes. What liberation theology adds to this reaction is that God is paradoxically

---

[12] Ibid., 32.

[13] David Tracy uses the category of fragment to describe how particular events or situations break open universalistic thinking and interrupt an essentialist imagination. They fragment every totality system. A negative experience of contrast grasps the interruption. "In the course of fragmenting all closed totalities, the most powerful fragments also show themselves not as substances but as events and positively open to liminal Infinity" (David Tracy, *Fragments: The Existential Situation of Our Time* [Chicago: University of Chicago Press, 2020], 1).

[14] Various liberation theologians use the term *liberation* with the same personal, social, and eschatological dimensions that characterize the traditional symbol of *salvation.*

revealed in this situation of suffering as the ground for resisting it by validating human life. God appears as the ultimate motive for negating the negation and as the basis of hope in an immediate and the ultimate future.

The bond between theology and ethics was introduced earlier as a common commandment in Jewish, Christian, and Muslim faith to love God and love the neighbor. Negative experience shows how the two commandments are inseparable and mutually entail each other.[15] In love of God one loves God's intimate friends; and in loving God's friends, one implicitly loves their creator.[16] The word *love* here has to be drained of its sentimental connotations. The issue engages value and respect for individual selfhood and active assistance to those in need. The merging of the two commandments calls up in its turn three basic principles that are simultaneously theological and ethical. First, the response to suffering and to negativity is resistance. This is God's will because God's love admits of no alternative. Second, this is a personal and a social principle; the community is called to this resistance. And, third, this resistance takes the form of action that is self-fulfilling. In other words, the resistance, the exercise of freedom against human suffering, creates actual meaning and value. These terse formulas will become meaningful in the section that follows.

These reflections on the nature and method of theology and its relation to ethics respond to cosmic pessimism on a theoretical and practical level. Liberation theologies are simultaneously apologetic and practical. They explain theology as rooted in a quest for ultimate liberation. Liberation represents salvation; it means human fulfillment. The orientation of human existence toward liberation grounds Christian faith and makes theology a humanistic discipline. Liberation

---

[15] Karl Rahner, "Reflections on the Unity of the Love of Neighbor and the Love of God," in *Theological Investigations,* vol. 6 (Baltimore: Helicon Press, 1969), 231–49.

[16] The following chapter on creation will offer a fuller account of God's love for God's creation. But at this point one can appreciate that God's infinite love is not divisible or mitigated by the plurality of creatures. God loves no single creature more or less because of God's love for others.

theologies make theology a practical discipline by addressing human suffering and those who feel the temptation to pessimism in this disordered world. They achieve their credibility by their application to real situations and the action they evoke.

The Logic of Liberation Theologies

Liberation theologies address specific forms of collective human oppression and suffering. As contextual theologies they respond to different kinds of social discrimination. But they share a common structure. All of them can be understood as growing out of social and cultural negative experiences of contrast that affect society and the faith community. Although liberation theologies often appear applicable to particular groups in society, they actually involve everyone in various roles and modes of participation. It is far more accurate to regard liberation theologies as specific instances of the intrinsic dynamics of all Christian theology rather than as identity theologies, departures from some neutral mainstream. When theology does not have within its ken the situation of the whole community, it cannot provide an adequate or coherent response to the temptations of cosmic pessimism.

This section illustrates the liberationist character of Christian theology by considering two examples drawn from different parts of the world. In each case the focus falls on one particular theologian who represents a movement. The first is the black liberation theology of James Cone, who was affected by the civil rights movement in the United States during the 1960s. The second is the liberation theology of Gustavo Gutiérrez who, following the urging of the Second Vatican Council, deliberately sought to address the desperate situation of the suffering masses of poor people in Latin America in the 1960s. These two outlines of developed theologies seek to show the logic of liberation theology. The portraits limit the treatment of theological content to the concept of God and the human before God. But these theologies draw out a logic that is indigenous to all Christian theology.

The Black Liberation Theology of James Cone

In his memoir, completed just before his death in 2018, James Cone describes how he came to write *A Black Theology of Liberation*.[17] Cone was engaged during the 1960s in a massive social tide demanding civil rights for black Americans led by Martin Luther King Jr. Early on in his memoir he recalls how friends urged him to write theology that directly addressed the situation. He recognized the necessity of the task, the sharp prophetic language it required, and his calling to it. "The black revolution that was exploding all over America needed a systematic theology. If I didn't do it, who would?"[18]

Beginning with context, all theology reflects some social perspective, and black liberation theology lies embedded in black experience. Cone decided to write theology for black people whose lives unfolded in a situation shaped by restrictive and intimidating social structures at every turn. His theology will never make complete sense without attention to the comprehensive racism of American culture and society. He wrote for blacks in a way that explicitly condemned racism and any theology that supported it. Cone's work thus carries an explicit tension between blacks and whites and aims at liberation from white supremacy. In a single society, people are always connected with one another. There can be no black theology that does not have a bearing on predominantly white society.

Cone had a clear sense of the structure of his theological thinking. He worked from three sources: black experience, scripture, and Jesus of Nazareth. "The black experience and scripture were my central sources for defining the meaning of Christian theology. Both were essential . . . but the black experience is the starting point."[19] The prevailing negative experience of black Americans directed attention to the stories of liberation of a people from Egyptian slavery and enabled Cone to compare the lynching of blacks to the death of Jesus

---

[17] James Cone, *A Black Theology of Liberation* (Philadelphia: Lippincott, 1970). Cone's memoir is *Said I Wasn't Gonna Tell Nobody: The Making of a Black Theologian* (Maryknoll, NY: Orbis Books, 2018).

[18] Cone, *Said I Wasn't Gonna Tell Nobody*, 56.

[19] Ibid., 66.

on the cross.[20] These are not decorative metaphors but frameworks for understanding black experience in a Christian way.

Turning now to the content of Cone's theology of God, his context supplies this question: how do we speak of God in a world of suffering due to oppression of blacks who are humiliated because they are black? Two principles govern the way he seeks responses: they must come from scripture, and they must depict "the God who is participating in the liberation of the oppressed in the land."[21] Cone's liberation theology of God touches the traditional predicates of God: God is creator, immanent and transcendent, and provident. But in each case the conception of God includes a message that supports black liberation: the revolutionary black movement attacks idolatrous structures; God is present within and participates in the movement toward freedom; God accompanies and supports black courage.

Cone explicitly addresses the implications of black theology for wider society. In a social body saturated in structural discrimination, where oppression is actual, God cannot be considered neutral. In these conditions God has to be on the side of the oppressed. God has made oppression of black people God's own condition: God is black. "Because God has made the goal of black people his own goal, Black Theology believes that it is not only appropriate but necessary to begin the doctrine of God with an insistence on his blackness."[22] God discriminates not against people but against oppression.

Finally, this black liberation theology promotes the use of political power; it solicits and empowers action in the direction of liberation from discriminating institutions. All theology points toward salvation, and, in this theology, salvation is liberation both in the here and now of persons freed from a thousand mechanisms of repression and in an ultimate future.

---

[20] James Cone, *The Cross and the Lynching Tree* (Maryknoll, NY: Orbis Books, 2011). Tracy captures the logic in the terms of fragments: "In African American thought, images seem quite naturally to become fragments that not only destroy all claims of totality [white supremacy] but also yield to fragments of hope, suggestions, redemption, infinity" (David Tracy, *Filaments: Theological Profiles* [Chicago: University of Chicago Press, 2020], 359).

[21] Cone, *A Black Theology of Liberation*, 116.

[22] Ibid., 121.

In sum, strong social critique runs through all of Cone's writing. His systematic theology is prophetic in character; it begins with critique of society, and no aspect of his constructive message lacks that critical edge. If all understanding is interpretation, and all interpretation springs from an implicit question, then all of Cone's theology has a basic hermeneutical structure that springs from his community's black experience in white America. The central logic of Cone's systematic theology is a desire to bring the full weight of Christian witness against the white supremacy that governs American life, society, and culture.

The Liberation Theology of Gustavo Gutiérrez

The theology of Gustavo Gutiérrez was first forged in Latin America during the 1960s, pushed by Vatican II's *Pastoral Constitution on the Church in the Modern World" (Gaudium et spes)*. In 1968, the Second General Conference of Latin American Bishops spoke of dire social inequality, dehumanizing poverty, structural injustice, and institutional violence that characterized peasant and urban life in South America. Gutiérrez was completely immersed in that world and actively participated in the newly awakened social consciousness. In 1969 he developed the idea of a theology of liberation, and two years later he published his classic text, *A Theology of Liberation.*[23]

Gutiérrez's theology of liberation began contextually; it was born out of the experience of the poor and his reflective engaged perception of life on the ground with students and in parish life in Lima, Peru. He was at home with the poor. One of the most moving descriptions of the poor of Latin America was formulated at the Bishops Conference in Puebla (1979) in terms of the faces of poverty's people: children, youth, indigenous people, peasants, laborers, the unemployed, marginalized, and elderly.[24] In Gutiérrez's theology, "the poor" functions as a symbol for a massively diverse

---

[23] Gustavo Gutiérrez, "Notes for a Liberation Theology," *Theological Studies* 31 (1970 [Spanish, 1969]): 243–61; idem, *A Theology of Liberation: History, Politics, and Salvation* (Maryknoll, NY: Orbis Books, 1973 [Spanish, 1971]).

[24] See Gustavo Gutiérrez, *The Power of the Poor in History* (Maryknoll, NY: Orbis Books, 1983), 133–34.

population spread through the region and points to people who have not chosen this condition but are captive to it. This poverty is degrading; it dehumanizes. The symbol "the poor" quickly became universal because the whole world found it meaningful.

The world of the poor sent Gutiérrez to scripture for the categories of theology, but not directly. Theological reflection must pass through immersion in life and praxis, a mixture of thought and participation in faith's active response to the negative situation. Theology is second, critical reflection, after and mediated through engagement with groups in the light of faith's practice. The problem for theology within the world of the poor is how to explain God to them. What better resource is there to reflect on the immense innocent suffering of the majority of people in Latin America than Job? Gutiérrez interprets the Book of Job as telling us that God's freedom and love establish human freedom and respect it by giving it the task of establishing justice on earth.[25]

But who is God in Gutiérrez's liberation theology? In a word, God is savior. The whole biblical story testifies to it. But the symbol for salvation in today's world must be liberation. Like all symbols, the idea of liberation is deep and layered. Saving liberation is first of all God creating the free human spirit that can act with autonomy. It also includes political emancipation—the possibility of, and the charge to construct, a society where people flourish. Further, liberation describes being in relation to God and being recreated from within by this relationship. Finally, liberation promises an absolute future of fulfillment.[26] In the end, God in Gutiérrez's theology is liberator in whom creation and salvation cohere. In this world God's liberation aims at embracing most intensely those who need it most desperately.

Gutiérrez discusses how this orientation of the gospel message toward the poor has implications for the whole church, not to mention society itself. The idea of the option for the poor, revised as a "preferential" option, expressly deals with this issue. But is not God

---

[25] Gustavo Gutiérrez, *On Job: God-Talk and the Suffering of the Innocent* (Maryknoll, NY: Orbis Books, 1987), 67–81.

[26] Gutiérrez, *A Theology of Liberation*, 153–68.

the God of all? His response to this objection is clear: the option for the poor describes God's attitude as represented in the teaching of Jesus about the neighbor. The neighbor is precisely the "other" or the "different," the one left by the side of the road.[27] In other words, on its deepest level, the option of the poor belongs especially to those who enjoy freedom and power. It is a choice for the whole church and all of society. Of course, it cuts across the interests of those whose wealth and power afflict the poor.

From beginning to end Gutiérrez's theology of liberation is activist. As an engaged theology, it begins with the reflective, intentional activity for liberation that he calls praxis. The resultant theological reflection is geared to fill what may be secular action for social justice with the power of the gospel. In fact, Gutiérrez's theology draws into itself a public movement for justice and completes it with spirituality in a full, metaphysical sense of doing God's will and fulfilling God's purpose in history. Gutiérrez also considers this activist spirituality as fulfilling the personal spiritual needs of all who participate in it.

The liberation theologies of Cone and Gutiérrez are not the same; they respond to very different historical contexts. Each theologian generated his liberationist understanding of Christianity independently of the other on two linguistically and culturally different territories. Yet the logic of how each understands Christianity resembles the other in a remarkable way. The structure that holds them together includes a negative experience of contrast and an ethical drive. Both theologies respond to a death-dealing social situation. It is known to be evil by those who are its victims and by any fair-minded observer. Its sinful character appears vividly against the background of the vision of reality supplied by the Christian faith tradition. The negative situation and the positive view of God as revealed in the ministry of Jesus of Nazareth supply a metaphysical motivation to act against the structural sin. The negativity of situations behind these two liberation theologies bears no less discouraging power than any found in human history. And yet these theologies record

---

[27] Gutiérrez, *The Power of the Poor in History*, 44, 50, 52.

another power that turns pessimism into opportunity to make meaning and create value.

Theology as a Practical, Humanistic, and Pluralistic Academic Discipline

Liberation theologies, as exemplified in Cone and Gutiérrez, may be compared and contrasted. But the analogy of their structures bears an indelible message. These, and so many other liberation theologies, should not be reduced to theologies defined by particular identities. They do not compete with each other but reveal a common negative dimension of historical existence and a positive source of power to resist it. This constitutes an intrinsic dimension of the discipline of Christian theology. Beneath all liberation theologies lies the contrast between death and life. God is a God of life; God stands opposed to the forces of death. The thread of coherence that runs from a negative experience of contrast through the critical method of liberation theologies reflects the structure of human existence itself. All Christian theology has to be liberationist to be faithful to the gospel and to be credible as a reflection of the human spirit in the face of cosmic pessimism.

Theology is an academic discipline because it operates at a critical reflective level. It consists of second-level language, the fruit of opening up the spontaneous views of the faith community to the scrutiny of other forms of knowledge. This does not rob faith of its autonomy. It generates its own form of knowledge. Religious beliefs cannot be reduced to the empiricism and mathematicization of the physical sciences any more than can other human sciences, despite some contrary efforts. But theology asks the epistemological and social critical questions of the meaningfulness of its language. Theology does not necessarily overcome metaphysical skepticism, but it shows that the skeptic's response to reality is itself a disposition of faith.

Theology is a pluralistic discipline; pluralism reigns both inside each faith tradition and among the religions. No universal theology can absorb the others without remainder inside the Christian communion of churches because of the historicist and perspectival character of faith traditions. The fragmentary character of reality cannot be overcome. The pluralism of faith traditions is historically necessary. But this positive rather than negative condition opens up a dialogical or conversational approach to ultimate reality and to learning more about it from other particular faiths. Pluralism rather than relativism describes the religious response to the question of ultimate reality and of human existence itself. The pluralism of a theological interpretation of reality does not undermine its objective academic status any more than the study of Plato, or Aristotle, or Wittgenstein fails to qualify as philosophy. Theology cannot really defeat a faith in ultimate agnosticism and relativism, but it offers the alternative of pluralism that is infinitely more satisfying.

Theology is a practical humanist discipline because of its ethical character. Although theology has an inherently metaphysical base, because it responds to ultimacy on the basis of revelatory historical mediation, the ultimate at theology's source cannot be separated from the grounding of ethics. Theology raises the questions that the empirical sciences cannot entertain: what is ultimate reality and what does it demand of us? Theology deals with human existence in terms of ultimacy and value. The ultimate in its turn cannot be separated from the concrete systems that structure social human existence. In Christian theology, God both makes demands and holds out liberation and justice as things to strive for. A practical theology cannot simply displace pessimism; pessimism has too much evidence to support it. But like the gratuity of revelation itself, God can activate a desire to create value and communicate a new sense of a positive destiny underlying human existence.

Part Three

The Content of
Christian Theology:
Basic Beliefs

5

God as Creator

This chapter begins three discussions that outline the content of Christian theology. They introduce God as creator, Jesus of Nazareth as mediator of God, and God as Spirit. More than half of the discussion up to this time has been dedicated to the boundaries that define the scope of theology. Limiting Christian beliefs to three doctrines does not allow expansive reflection on the subject matter of the symbols of faith. But the whole discussion intends no more than an introduction to the discipline that analyzes these teachings in greater detail. The three doctrines together represent the core of Christian belief. Although the treatment of each teaching is far from comprehensive, it touches on essential elements of the tradition. The intent is ecumenical rather than attention to a particular Christian denomination. This presentation also qualifies as constructive theology, and this means that the categories reviewed here involve interpretation that the context described in the earlier parts of the book requires.

Science and theology both offer comprehensive views of reality—they meet at the juncture of a vision of the whole. Both the consideration of the universe in terms of material process and laws of nature and the doctrine of creation provide a macro-vision of the whole "from the beginning." The first chapter listed science as one of the factors that have turned the imagination toward a critical demand for evidence in interpreting the world. Scientific criticism often finds popular religion an easy target for skepticism. But the constructive side of science, which offers new penetrating insight into the universe and human beings in it, also has a large positive impact on the theological imagination. While science should not transgress into the field of transcendent metaphysics, it nonetheless offers principles that theology cannot ignore. More constructively, some of them help define the context that forms the framework of credibility for religious beliefs. Three suppositions reinforce the way science has influenced the context for the reflections on creation that follow.

A first supposition is the premise that the reality of the world and the whole universe has to be understood developmentally, that is, as a process of becoming. Everything is in motion. Whether in the sphere of cosmogenesis or the evolution of life, reality consists of movement constituted by time. The nature of finite being entails the continuing emergence of our universe from some initiating set of conditions. Being is becoming.

A second supposition may be less convincing for religious traditions, but for many it alters faith's perception. It maintains that God does not intervene intermittently into the web of interaction that structures what is ordinarily called nature. Science in a sense presupposes this for lack of evidence, but, from a theological perspective, the transcendence of God prevents the imagination from reducing God's action to finite categories. God does not perform a finite function within the created universe because God as creator remains altogether another kind of dynamism.

The third supposition takes the form of a challenge: the doctrine of creation must be such that it disallows a perception or an understanding of God being discovered as an element of the material universe. But at the same time, God cannot be "posited" as exclusively above or outside of the universe but as also inside it. Without some real connection with human existence, which is part of the world, there would be no grounds for speaking about God. The doctrine of creation fits within these parameters. Science thus appears as a positive influence in theology by setting the context for constructive understanding of God in relation to the world. The doctrine of creation learns from science. But, as theology, the doctrine of creation transcends science with mystical intent. And the place of science moves from being a source of disenchantment to becoming a positive guide for theological reflection.

The reflection on the doctrine of creation will also incorporate other principles established in earlier chapters. In contrast to the premises of skepticism, the very idea of God implies transcendence; God has to be recognized as other than any limited physical thing that is imaginable. The permanent tendency militating against coherent discussions of God lies in anthropomorphism, a kind of predication that reduces God to creaturely dimensions. Paradoxically, the transcendence of God postulates God's immanence. But God's immanence excludes the possibility of limiting God in space or time and maintains that God suffuses all reality, penetrating the world and each creature. God is not "up there" or "out there" beyond an expanding universe, but within it without being a part of it. Also, the previous chapter dwelt on faith's conviction that God communicates life and liberation. The theology of creation has to account for these convictions that are contained in Christian teaching.

This short introduction to the theology of creation cannot meet the richness and depth of the subject matter. It remains restricted to a standard set of central elements that constitute the main lines of the doctrine. They form the spine of the chapter and include the negative logic of Dionysius that God has no name and can only be affirmed as beyond all our conceptions. God also has to be thought of in terms of activity rather than as a substance or subject, as energy rather than as a being, in order to be immanent to creation. The theological analysis of the idea that God creates out of nothing helps to build some understanding around the absolute mystery that surrounds this paradoxical doctrine. Two last points attached to the Christian understanding of God are continual creation and providence. The one shows why creation was not a past event but is an ongoing "activity" or "act" of God, and the other shows how this implies a doctrine of God's care for the world. Both of these points need careful interpretation in our time.

Finally, the presentation of these key elements of the idea of creation are shaped by a thesis that guides the interpretation. The doctrine of creation shows that a strong and appropriate metaphor for speaking of God is *Presence.* Presence includes within itself the creating power and sovereignty of God implied in creating and at the same time the idea that God is provident, attending to creation, and accompanying it with care. It remains to be shown whether this synthetic idea both illumines and is justified by the basic theological elements of the doctrine.

Thinking of God Who Has No Name

Moses asked God's name of the voice from the burning bush, and God answered, "I am who I am" (Ex 3:14). Many are the interpretations of what that meant in the past and what it means today. But many would agree that the no-name functions as a symbol of God's transcendence: no name can be applied to God because God infinitely exceeds all predicates. A good place to begin a theology of creation is with a descriptive account of the religious consciousness that accounts for the doctrine, for that experience includes the theme of God's transcendence.

Speaking about God always presumes that God is not part of the world. To be God, God must infinitely surpass everything and all things cumulatively: the world, the universe(s), or simply all finite reality.[1] The subtle rule of affirmation about God proposed by Dionysius, involving a negation of the "earthly" meaning of all terms when applied to God, protects God's transcendence. And yet human beings experience God within themselves and by extension within the world. Faith traditions include people who freely speak of God on the recognition that the language must be dialectical or self-negating. God exceeds the implicit anthropomorphism involved in the language.

The privileged metaphor for speaking of God in this work is Presence. It is usually capitalized when used as a substantive and a name for God even though the correspondence cannot be literal. The very speaking about God entails referential language. One of the

---

[1] There are alternatives to this view that depict God as "part" of reality. What is presented here affirms God's absolute transcendence and immanence dialectically.

positive features of the term *presence* lies in its vagueness about how that "presence" is experienced and how it applies to God. The term has a diffuseness that allows many different ways in which "Presence" could manifest itself or be perceived. The different modes of recognition, in turn, open up different aspects of "Presence" itself. Medieval theologians generally accepted Dionysius's rule that anything assigned to God as a quality had to be denied as doing so with literal accuracy. Language about God is strictly dialectical; God is in no way like we imagine. "Presence" applied to God protects God's transcendence by being both dialectical in the way it refers to God and deliberately vague about the way that Presence manifests itself. At bottom, the term "Presence" should not be regarded as a name referring to a substance or in any way defining, but as a symbolic mechanism that invites the imagination to "pass through" the term and recognize that what is referred to cannot be named.

The name of Dionysius is well known in the practice of contemplative prayer and the disciplines that study mysticism. Buddhists and Christian mystics appreciate his language. It is important to recognize that when theology explicitly turns to the subject matter of God, it has entered the mystical dimensions of faith experience. The "mystical" and "mysticism" should not be regarded as representing a sphere that is utterly different from ordinary religious experience and consciousness. At best, the continuity and distinction can only be measured by dedication and intensity. In the end, the terms "God" and "creation" are mystical symbols. In Dionysius's thinking, these symbols operated by representing a sphere that is transcendent; they invite the mind to "ascend" into the heights of an expansive world of being in contrast with the world of immediacy and fact. Our time demands a repositioning of that structure: we have to preserve this dialectical tension, but today's scientific worldview requires that we also find transcendent reality within the physical world, not above it. God utterly transcends material finitude but does so by being absolutely other than the physical world and being present within it. Rather than thinking of this mysticism as available only to practiced religious professionals, the mystical refers to a dimension of human experience that is potentially available to all human beings as an experience of transcendence. The point here, once again, goes to the deep dimensions of human experience that support all theological language and creation language in particular.

The symbol of God as Presence, as transcendent presence without a name, absorbs without cancelling other symbols for God. God as activity carries a potential for explaining how God can be immanent within creation but distinct from the autonomous identity of creatures. This idea of God as pure act or action provides a basis for Thomas Aquinas's penetrating analysis of God's immanence in the world. God is the pure act and source of being. When Paul Tillich calls God the "ground" of being, his thinking comes close to the mystic Meister Eckhart's conception of an inner divine power sustaining all existent things. The divine is inside, at the center of the real. The contemporary idea that God can be symbolized by the dynamic abstraction "creativity" allowed Gordon Kaufman to speak about God within an evolutionary framework as a dynamism that combines randomness and order and drives all reality. Karl Rahner shifted the framework for speaking about God with objective symbolic terms and designated God in terms of human understanding with the phrase "absolute incomprehensible mystery." The symbol combines two perspectives on God: God is absolute mystery because God is transcendent reality; God appears in human consciousness as a mysterious dimension that intrinsically surpasses all understanding.[2]

Presence as a symbol of God does not compete with these attempts at giving God a name that exceeds all names. All of these and so many more symbols for ultimate reality are compatible with Presence, which draws up into itself other facets of God's being and God's mediated manifestation in consciousness.

God as Activity

God relates to the world and human existence primarily through God's creating. This and the next section take up the experience that allows talk about God as creator in two stages. The first analyzes

---

[2] These symbols for God are developed in Roger Haight, *Faith and Evolution: A Grace-Filled Naturalism* (Maryknoll, NY: Orbis Books, 2019), 63–70.

how the experience of being absolutely dependent on God generates the idea of God creating the self and the world. The following
section then analyzes the idea of creation itself. These topics help
to clarify the inner rationale for a theistic understanding of reality.

A description of the experience of God as creator presupposes
insights that have already been discussed. It builds on the principle
that human beings primarily experience God within the self rather
than as something objective and out there. This does not mean that
God does not "appear" as real or other than the self, but that God
is encountered impacting human subjectivity. Another refinement
notes how God thus encountered relates to the self: revelation of
God includes revelation of the self in relation to God and God to the
self. God does not displace or "take over" the self; God as Presence
is more like an action or energy that sustains the self rather than
being over against the self. The discussion of non-duality assumes
importance at this point.

Against the background of these ideas, what can be said of the
experience or religious consciousness that grounds the understanding
that God is creator? A first response transpires on the level of ordinary
religious experience of the power and order of the universe. The
second offers a critical analysis of the structure of that experience.

To begin, there is no "standard" experience of God. Every such
experience will be different. But the objective world as we find it
offers a place to locate the possible mediation of a basic experience of God as creator. John Calvin, who had an extraordinary
sense of the sovereignty of God, offers an incisive description of
the experience of many. He taught explicitly that the first book of
revelation consists of the magnificent order of the universe and the
natural world. God is revealed in the created world; creation offers
visible manifestations of the invisible God. The workmanship of the
universe shines forth the glory of its author. The universe communicates a knowledge of God's power, intelligence, and goodness in
its coherence and order if one reads it by faith. Calvin cites Psalm
104, a prayerful descriptive story of creation, to show that the order
of nature manifests God. The hidden God gleams in the wonderfully
interwoven mechanisms of nature, when they are read by the eyes of
faith. The world of nature is awesome, and it invites contemplative

appreciation and delight in the works of God that are displayed in the beautiful theater of nature.[3]

The witness of Calvin invites two comments. First, he is in most respects a premodern religious thinker who readily sees the world as saturated with God's power on the macro level. But science can help people today retrieve his sense of enchanted awe relative to the size, intricacy, and beauty in the emergent complexity found in the physical, chemical, and molecular structure of the universe. This is not a matter of argument but of intelligent aesthetic response that is alert to order and gratuitousness, the interplay of random creativity and beauty. The second notes that Calvin's attention to the breadth of nature does not distract from the fact that any particular situation, person, or event can mediate revelation in a point of time. Revelation always takes place in particular times and places, but it never escapes the mediating sphere of this world.

This first level of ordinary religious experience of creation can be a source for a dynamic spiritual response. Calvin confessed that he thought that God created all things for the sake of human beings, intending creation for each person's human flourishing. "God has destined all things for our good and salvation but at the same time to feel his power and grace in ourselves and in the great benefits he has conferred upon us, and so bestir ourselves to trust, invoke, praise, and love him."[4] Ignatius of Loyola shared the same sentiment in his *Spiritual Exercises:* God gifts human beings with creation, dwells in creation and in each person, and "labors and works for me in all the creatures on the face of the earth."[5] Both of them exhibit a strong sense of an intentional presence of God mediated through the process of creation to each human being, one that sets up a response of dialogue and a return of love through a way of life.

Friedrich Schleiermacher, as was noted in Chapter 2, subjects the ordinary conviction that we exist in a relationship with God to critical

---

[3] John Calvin, *Institutes of the Christian Religion*, ed. John T. McNeill (Philadelphia: Westminster Press, 1960), 1.5.14, also 1.14.20. The context here is not a search for a proof of the existence of God.

[4] Ibid., 1.14.22.

[5] Ignatius of Loyola, *The Spiritual Exercises of Saint Ignatius*, ed. George E. Ganss (St. Louis: The Institute of Jesuit Sources, 1992), Paras. 234–36.

analysis.[6] The experience of being in an absolute relationship of dependence on God is not a particular experience, but a deep structure in all religious experiences. The framework of this conception lies in a reflection upon the self as a being that is consciously present to itself while being simultaneously present to the world around it. In all its exchanges with the world, human existence, or the human person, is both passive and active, receptive and responsive. This passion-action dynamic describes the inner resources of freedom. In all cases humans receive from and act upon the world. But it is strikingly the case that, relative to the whole of personal existence and activity as such, the human person is absolutely dependent in being. Human beings are responsible for their actions in the world, but they are not responsible for, but passive relative to, their very existence. Human existence arises from a source other than the self, to which it relates as being absolutely dependent.

The status of this structure of experience bears more significance than any particular instance of it in an experience of God with a specific character such as awe, reverence, gratitude, loyalty, or love. This inner dynamic describes a universal characteristic of human existence. Moreover, it contains the grounds for recognizing further dimensions that the relationship of absolute dependence implies or entails. For example, this relationship of absolute dependence contains the source for recognizing the meaning of the term *God*. Being conscious of an absolute relationship of dependence and being conscious of God are the same thing. One can define the meaning of the term *God* as being that on whom one exists in an absolute relationship of dependence. Creation itself, in the objective sense of all that is created, can be defined as that which is because of its absolute dependence upon God. In other words, this deep structure of human reflective being-present-to-the-self, in recognizing its absolute dependence in being, accounts for all God-consciousness. And because the self is part of the world, a part that can be described as the world conscious of itself, this absolute dependence on God entails all temporal existence. The structure of the world is revealed in the

---

[6] This and the next paragraph are drawn from Friedrich Schleiermacher, *The Christian Faith* (London: Bloomsbury T&T Clark, 2016), #3 (pp. 12–18).

structure of the self standing before God in absolute dependence. The doctrine of creation has its roots in the deep structure of human self-consciousness and world-consciousness. The inner structure of the experience of the self accounts as well for the revelation of and the testimony to the creation-consciousness found in scripture.

Another dimension of Schleiermacher's analysis of the roots of the doctrine of creation in religious consciousness deserves notice. In some respects his analysis looks like conceptual sleight of hand that is then projected on reality. But he was an epistemological realist; the experience of absolute dependence is experience of God being present to human reflection. It is not "direct" experience but mediated through self- and world-consciousness. But it allows the experience of absolute dependence to refer as well to God's absolute causality, which is referred to as active omnipotence. The ground of the experience of absolute dependence is the absolute causality of God, and it extends to the whole order of nature and the universe. One could also think of God's absolute causality as the absolute vitality of the world. The basic answer to the question of what God does in the world is that God creates; creating vitality is God's activity.[7]

Creation out of Nothing

In theology, creation generally means to make something out of nothing. This active sense of the term, a performance, has only God as its subject or agent. Creation also has a second objective sense: creation is what God creates. In this sense, creation refers to the whole of reality. Everything apart from God is creation.

What the idea of God creating refers to is an absolute mystery. If God is inherently unknowable mystery, then God's action too has to be absolutely mysterious. Sometimes this gets reduced to something like being too big to imagine, especially today when the size and age of the universe(s) blows open imaginative efforts to grasp them. But

---

[7] Ibid., #52, pp. 200–203. Note that the causality that is predicated of God transcends all human perceptions and conceptions of causality. It too remains mystery.

the mystery involved in the doctrines of God and creation cannot be reduced to a matter of quantity; *mystery* is a technical theological term that refers to God as transcendent: absolute difference in kind from everything else. Unlike a problem that has a solution, mystery remains intrinsically incomprehensible.

The point of this section is to move more deeply into the idea of creation itself and what it entails, as these have been developed in the theological tradition. The doctrine suffers from being both overlooked and misunderstood, especially when Christian theology interacts with science on the question of how God acts in the world. The idea of creation defines the basic relationship between God and the world, and in so doing it serves as a grounding for other important Christian conceptions.

The phrase "out of nothing" distinguishes God's action from other forms of bringing something new into existence. It is not clear whether this idea exists in scripture, even though translations sometimes use the phrase. The dominant scriptural metaphor has God's power injecting order and intelligibility into some primordial chaos or unordered flow. "The earth was without form and void . . . and the Spirit of God was moving over the face of the waters" (Gen 1:2). Because the idea of nothing can only have meaning by negation, it is easy to see how imaginative metaphors predominated. Creation consisted of injecting definite shape and organic order into chaos. The idea of creation out of a more literal "nothing" arose from critical reflection. In a transcendent monotheism, where God creates everything, God logically has to preexist everything else.

God creating seems to involve God causing something to be, since the causal connection between things is one of the most common of human experience. But the many forms of everyday causation we witness in our world differ entirely from the causality exercised by God. God is not a distinct finite entity. God is not a something, not a subject, but is depicted as transcendent and immanent by pure activity. Speaking of God creating out of nothing leads the discussion into a metaphysical sphere. Saying God does not make by using existent material moves the discussion into a qualitatively different and unimaginable framework. This point is crucial to our inability to understand what it means to say that God creates. It has no analogue, no example, and all examples that try to explain how God causes are mistaken or misleading.

Recognizing that God's creative action is transcendent and incomparable to the agency and effectiveness of all finite causality is crucial for clarifying to some degree God's relationship to the world, at least negatively in its distinction from intra-worldly activity. God creates the "to be" of finite reality; God sustains it in being as semi-autonomous finite agents that are themselves created agents; but God is not a creature and thus does not act in a creaturely way. All finite beings and operations in the world, therefore, are actively being created by God, who creates by holding them in existence; by sustaining finite being and agency God participates in earthly activity but as sustainer in being rather than as finite agent.

This subtle relationship between God's creating agency and this-worldly processes is explained by Thomas Aquinas where he describes how God and finite agents can be co-producers of new forms of being. What follows digests a classic statement of his vision of how God acts in the world.[8] He begins by setting up the problem of how God can act in a system of interrelated vectors of force or what he calls causes: "For it does not seem possible for one action to proceed from two agents. So, if the action whereby a natural effect is produced proceeds from a natural body, it does not proceed from God." He then introduces the principle by which he will resolve the problem: "In every agent, in fact, there are two things to consider: namely, the thing itself that acts, and the power by which it acts."

To illustrate this duality, he looks at an agent employing an instrument, as a carpenter uses a hammer: "The power of a lower agent depends on the power of the superior agent, according as the superior agent gives this power to the lower agent whereby it may act; or preserves it; or even applies it to the action, as the artisan applies an instrument to its proper effect." "And just as the lowest agent is found immediately active [hammer on nail], so also is

---

[8] This paragraph summarizes Thomas Aquinas, *Summa contra Gentiles*, Book III, Chapter 70, entitled "How the same effect is from God and from a natural agent."

the power of the primary agent [carpenter] found immediate in the production of the effect."

On that analogy, he resolves the problem of dual agency in this way: "It is not inappropriate for the same effect to be produced by a lower agent and God: by both immediately, though in different ways." And more fully:

It is also apparent that the same effect is not attributed to a natural cause and to divine power in such a way that it is partly done by God, and partly by the natural agent; rather, it is wholly done by both, according to a different way, just as the same effect is wholly attributed to the instrument and also wholly to the principal agent.

This metaphysical conception may be paraphrased in a less Scholastic way. God acts in the world by creating, by holding everything other than God, from an electron and its motion, to a human person and a black hole, in existence. This refers to its being, in contrast to nothingness or nonbeing. It also means that God is not simply active in a general way, holding the whole in existence, but that divine power extends to and encompasses every particular thing and event. In so doing, God's creating activity provides the possibility and the existing of the operation of the whole system and every element in it. This conception transforms the conception of how God is found in particular events and in so-called special revealing events in history. God does not intervene because God is always present to each particular thing. As cosmologist William Stoeger puts it, one should understand "special divine actions as richly differentiated modes or expressions of God's universal creative action."[9]

Creation out of nothing contains the rationale for God's immediate presence to everything: God is not separable from God's action. God

---

[9] William Stoeger, SJ, "Conceiving Divine Action in a Dynamic Universe," *Scientific Perspectives on Divine Action: Twenty Years of Challenge and Progress*, ed. Robert John Russell et al. (Berkeley, CA: The Center for Theology and the Natural Sciences; Vatican City: Vatican Observatory Publications, 2008), 246–47, 240.

is God's action. Creation makes God present to all that exists in a relationship and union that is incomparable and incomprehensible. No union could possibly be closer, so that the idea of non-duality is particularly apt at this point. The world and God are not the same: God is not the world, nor the world God. But the world only exists because God is present to it creating its being.

Up to this point, creation has referred to the activity of God creating. When the term *creation* is shifted to refer objectively to that which is created, the term means everything, the whole world. In this frame of reference one can speak of creation as God making the world "out of everything." From the human perspective of being part of the objective world, God creates everything out of everything else. God is the prime agent behind emergence and evolution; God holds the whole network of interbeing together; God is at work within the flow of forces that mathematical algorithms describe in order to explain why things happen. God is always the "prime" agent holding the finite agents and their motions in being. Both the complete distinction between and the unity of the agents contained in this framework, held together in tension, help to sort out this mysterious relationship. Aquinas used a simpler Aristotelian language than the physical and biological sciences allow today. The term *causality* is semantically too blunt to function in the complex variations of scientific observation. The compressed narratives contained in scientific algorithms describe the measured flow of reality, the interconnectedness of variables influencing other variables that can be repeated. Science quantifies and compares the ongoing interconnections between things. God's causality is not a part in the puzzle, but the transcendent power and presence creating what transpires and holding everything together in interdependent existence.

Finally, this whole vision can be referred to as *panentheism.* This term is etymologically literal: everything exists within the embrace of the power of God; God is within all that happens. These reciprocal relationships, however, are not really understood because they refer to incomprehensible divine activity. And that's the point: to not confuse God's being and action with that of the world.

Continual Creation

Continual creation and the following section on providence are, practically speaking, corollaries of the idea of creation. Continual creation simply affirms that God's creating should not be conceived as a single action in the past that brought the world into existence to be left running as an autonomous machine. Instead, creation is ongoing: all existing things are being created at all times, because they are held in being against nothingness at every moment of their existence. From a human perspective, therefore, it appears that God creates continuously across time, and thus the doctrine of continual creation.

But this way of thinking about creation requires some more refinement. Thinking of God creating as an ongoing activity depicts God creating from the human viewpoint of being in time. This perspectival statement thus depicts God acting as God performing an action in time. But God is neither within time nor subject to time but the creator of time. From the perspective of God, which is unimaginable but only projected from the negation of God as subject to time, God's act of creation is better thought of as a simple act outside of time.[10] The eternal act of God's being and creating is *totum simul*—everything all at once. God's eternity means that everything that was, is, and will be, the whole of it and in its discrete elements, is contained within the being and power of God all at once as an eternal present.

This classical analysis of the implications of the doctrine of creation holds up in a modern phenomenology of the roots of the doctrine in a religious consciousness of being absolutely dependent. The dependence has both a metaphysical and a physical dimension; human beings are both absolutely dependent and historically dependent through the myriad relationships with the world studied by particle physics, molecular chemistry, higher biological complexities, psychology, and reflectively conscious social relationships. But it is

---

[10] It should be expressly noted that one can say that God is both outside and inside of time and space because the register or field of meaning for God completely transcends finitude and is incomprehensibly other.

the absolute metaphysical dependence that generates the doctrine of creation. Absolute dependence does not exclude temporal dependence but includes it. All things are both temporally and absolutely dependent on God's creating. Conscious dependence of finite being provides the experiential basis for the idea of creation. The doctrine of creation, therefore, does not refer to temporal beginning but to the relationship of all finite being to its source and ground of being. In itself, the doctrine of creation does not answer the question of whether there was a "non-time" when God was not creator.

Providence

The idea that God is provident also flows out of the doctrine of continual creation as an almost logical entailment. But analysis of the connections helps unravel the nest of interrelated dimensions of the Christian conception of creation out of nothing.

A first explosive relation between two ideas is the connection of God's continual presence to what God creates and the idea that God is personal. The first idea is straightforward: the absolute Presence of creating power puts God within all being. God is God's action, and God is where God acts. God is the "within" of all that is. But God is also personal. It is not possible to affirm God as the creator of all that is and at the same time think that God lacks any of the quality or capacity of being that God has created. As noted earlier, God cannot be restricted to the dimensions of a being or able to be measured by the finite reality of this world. But neither can God be less than the possessor of the qualities that human beings know and enjoy. The standard way of symbolizing this says that God is personal while maintaining that God is not a person in the limited individual mode of human personhood. "God is personal" means that God's presence is encountered by human subjects in a way that includes intelligence and intentionality while not reducing God to being a person in the way we experience persons. The creator God knows and loves what is God's own in an unimaginably transcendent way.

The combination of thinking of God as both creator and personal spontaneously generates the idea of God as provident. Providence refers to the protective care that God has for what God has created. Belief in God's providence translates God's literal "fore-seeing" into love, attention, and safekeeping of what God has created. It would be hard to conceive how anything less than God's love and concern for what God creates could be the determining motive for creation itself. On the premise that God must love what God creates, Christian theology almost takes for granted this basic conviction that runs through both Old and New Testaments of scripture. God loves the world; God is for life and the fullness of existence.

The joining of the doctrine of the transcendent and immanent power of God and the doctrine of the personal love of God for the world in an anthropomorphic way leads to serious problems for religious consciousness. Chapter 1 described the so-called problem of evil, in which the actual course of evolution and history through death-dealing competition seems directly to attack the idea of God's creating power unfolding with loving concern and presence. Without fully addressing here the existential cosmic pessimism that works its way into present-day consciousness, something constructive has to be said about God's providence, which is so intimately attached to the idea of creation. Prior to addressing pessimism directly (in Chapter 7), one should have some framework for thinking about God's providence in a non-anthropomorphic way.

God's providence may be understood in a way that corresponds to God's transcendence and immanence within creation rather than in terms of an intervening into the course of human events. God's providence cannot be read off of the events of history as though God were the actor that determined finite events. In structural terms the problem here is analogous to reading God's revelation reductively in the literal terms of its media rather than recognizing that those media are symbols bearing witness to a transcendent reality other than themselves. God's providence should not be read as a special discrete action here and now, because God's general creating action includes every specific event. So too, God does not care for intelligent human beings by doing things for them, but by sustaining them in the use of the gifts and powers that the creator supports within them. The creative power makes all things dependent on God in their being, but their being contains within itself semi-autonomous potentials and powers for action. God acts by continuously sustaining those powers. Understanding God as another finite actor misunderstands God's transcendence and God's immanence. Praying to God to act in our interest by a specific finite action misinterprets how God acts in history.[11] God and God's action as creator of the world cannot be imagined as the action of a finite being acting in the world. The problem of evil confuses God's action with finite acting. By contrast, the idea of God creating us and sustaining us to do what we are able to do will play a major role in addressing pessimism with a positive and active view of creaturehood.

A stronger, more realistic, and incisive metaphor for providence, at least in our time, is contained in the idea of divine accompaniment. "God accompanying" combines a positive active conception of God being present with an active rather than a passive or neutral view of God's initiative and action. But God's accompaniment operates on a different plane than the one described by the algorithms of science. God within creation provides the power of being and action, and the metaphysical tendency for becoming, growth, and achievement of a fullness of the specific kind of being involved. God's accompanying action embraces the individuality of every actual being. God's act of creating enables and supports human creativity; finite creativity flows out of and cooperates with God's power of being in seeking immediate or longer-term goals.

Much more can be said about accompaniment and being accompanied. God's presence and cooperation lie open to the language of interpersonal exchange under the strict proviso of a denial and non-reduction of God's action to the level of creaturely work. The non-dual unity of God's creating presence and finite creaturely action require the single united agency of distinct vectors of action; God and human freedom and creativity work together. But God

---

[11] But praying to God in a time of distress is still meaningful. It expresses clearly one's dependence in existence; and it makes complete symbolic sense to put words around this meaning.

accompanies not by performing a distinct part of earthly or natural action; rather, everything that occurs in the universe "is wholly done by both, according to a different way."[12]

God's presence and action within the operations of the world correlate with what the Qur'an describes as God keeping an account of history. The idea of God recording the past undergoes a revision in the reflective light of the idea of God as an eternal presence to all that occurs in the universe. While God's paying attention surely instills a sense of responsibility and caution about the moral character of individual behavior and produces a salutary fear of God because of human proclivities, it also has a positive and moving consequence. God's eternal presence may also be expressed in terms of God's eternal memory of not only human faults but also of human virtue and achievement. The metaphor of memory in time, always struggling with forgetfulness, translates into the context of God's *semper simul* as God's ever-present simultaneous grounding and preserving what appears in time, even as history continually passes into finite nonexistence. God's overseeing reality actually transforms the ephemeral character of every individual thing into a field for generating permanent, indeed eternal, meaning.

Providence, especially when it is understood to entail God as personal creator, instills a hopeful confidence in God's ultimate care in an absolute future. More will be said about eschatology, the Christian understanding of the end of time, in the concluding chapter on the Christian life. But a fuller "image" of God revealed in the ministry of Jesus is discussed in the chapter that follows; it further instills an absolute confidence that, in spite of every setback in life, one can hope in an absolute future.

The idea of an absolute future within the sphere of God, who is the infinite power of being that transcends time in the *totum simul* of eternity, also suggests an already accomplished, or at least "envisioned," end time within the reality of God. Should human beings project such a finished state of affairs as already posited by divine eternity beyond time and beyond human imagination and striving? Or is reality in its present state, as process thinking insists, never

---

[12] Aquinas, *Summa contra Gentiles*, 3.70.

fully achieved and forever in process? It might be better to relegate such a question to what Calvin called God's secret plan of all reality where the human imagination cannot go. In fact, as a metaphysical doctrine, creation does not provide information. It simply builds a framework for positioning everything we know in relation to God. The conception of God creating out of nothing provides a sphere of absolute mystery that by definition transcends human inquiry.

This discussion of God represents a bare outline of some of the standard Christian teachings about "the creator of heaven and earth." That teaching crossed a threshold with the recognition that God creates out of nothing. That insight cancels the ability of the imagination, which clings to sensory images, to enter into any positive analysis of God's action. It also elevates God's transcendence to a universal and all-encompassing sphere. God is not the God of a people, or a world, or even a universe, but the immanent Presence of the absolute power that engenders reality itself. God actually obliterates all the tensions and paradoxes that attach to a particular idea of God and depict God from the human perspective of finitude and time: transcendent and immanent, immense and yet personal, universally relevant yet attentive to the individual. The conception of God as creator offers no universal system; it proposes God as the ratification of the individual; it saves the fragmentary and gives it standing. These tensions really arise from human inability to comprehend God's absolute transcendent mystery.

One of the clearest and most credible characterizations of God comes from the work of Karl Rahner who, as noted earlier, insisted on calling God the absolute incomprehensible mystery. "Mystery" in this usage does not refer to a problem that theoretically has a resolution, but to something intrinsically transcendent to any and all definition or analysis. The mystics enter into this sphere of wordlessness, and concepts like emptiness in Buddhism chase after it in a dialectical way. The term *transcendence* has lost its power to enforce the negation that it entails when referring to God. God as transcendence includes within itself not only creation but also salvation and its contemporary symbol, liberation. Nothing can be added to God creating that could possibly deepen or render closer the relationship of God as Presence to finite reality than God being its creator. The message of Jesus about that relationship, delivered largely in anthropomorphic terms, draws out in parable, aphorism, and action the implications for life within this primordial relationship.

6

Jesus Christ as Mediator

No area in Christian theology receives more attention than Christology, the discipline dedicated to understanding the person and role of Jesus Christ. A vast number of books appear each month from around the world. The differences among these publications is also surprising: they range by degrees from popular to technical; they express the views of different churches and denominations; they advocate for different groups; and they address different audiences. Christology is also a complicated discipline that comprises different specialties and, in effect, different sub-disciplines. An integral Christology must consult biblical Christology, the history of the discipline, its relation to other doctrines, the study of how Jesus saves (soteriology), dialogue with science, and consultation with other religions and their mediators. All these fields contribute essential reflection for the formulation of an adequate Christology.

This chapter on Jesus Christ cannot develop a full account of its subject matter. It has a precise aim of offering a clear analysis of some of the essential topics that help make up the christological framework of Christian faith. It intends to describe "the lay of the land." But because the discipline of Christology is pluralistic and the discussion refined, it requires a thematic overture on how the basic issues developed. The aim is to show how faith in Jesus Christ as mediator of Christian faith developed into a specialized discipline of study.

Jesus of Nazareth, a historical figure, became the central historical medium of Christian revelation. In the nineteenth century biblical scholars and theologians became interested in highlighting how Jesus of Nazareth actually appeared to his contemporaries. This requires careful investigation, because the gospel narratives are sometimes more faith-inspired hagiographic depictions of Jesus than critical-historical accounts of his actual ministry. If Jesus as a historical figure was the medium of Christian revelation, having an idea of what he actually taught and did becomes important to Christian theology. But this also means that Jesus's humanity is a given at the outset of the development of Christology; there is no indication that Jesus, during his ministry, was considered a personal divinity. Beginning Christology with the recognition that Jesus was a human being will serve as a basis of his ability to communicate universally with universal relevance.

With this background it then becomes important to formulate some synthetic understanding of Jesus's teaching. For a variety of different reasons the early church became so caught up in Jesus's standing as a divine figure, as God incarnate, that the actual teachings of Jesus were overshadowed by reflection on the sheer participation of God in the human condition. In an age of criticism and realism, going back to Jesus's teaching and his immediate destiny because of his teaching becomes important today.

There are indications that immediately after Jesus's arrest and execution, the disciples were left in disarray. But after a certain period of time they banded together to preach publicly that Jesus had been raised to life with God. The resurrection of Jesus bears a central pivotal importance in the interpretation of the person and role of Jesus as Christ or Messiah. Christology has to take a position on what Jesus's resurrection means and how the disciples came to affirm it. The discussion here will develop a realist position on Jesus's resurrection.

Closely related to Jesus's resurrection, the whole New Testament bears witness to the fact that Jesus was considered savior. But this was not expressed in a uniform matter. It becomes crucial to form a position on what it means to say that Jesus was experienced and construed as savior and to see the link between that experience of salvation in Jesus's name and the interpretation of him as a divine figure. The recognition of the divinity of Jesus is a direct function of the experience of salvation mediated through him.

In the final part of this chapter the discussion turns to a critical analysis of the development of a realist view of Jesus's divinity. How should the divinity of Jesus be understood today? These reflections on the divinity of Jesus Christ have to take into account the situation of religious pluralism, in which the varieties of religious traditions coexist in various urban centers of the world. How can Christian theology maintain the tradition of the divinity of Jesus and also honor the autonomous integrity of other religious traditions and mediations of ultimate reality? In all of this the accent falls not on the adequacy of the treatment in a short space but on the logic of how the elements fit together.

Finally, the discussion of these many components of an integral Christology unfolds in a present-day situation of religious plurality that seems to undercut the ultimacy or the specific truth of any one of them. Relativism does not liberate; it scatters and trivializes; it is not overcome by an attitude that judges that all religious traditions are either the same or equally true and thereby leveling differences. Pluralism means holding truth and difference together in a subtle higher framework that both affirms the truth that Jesus mediates ultimate reality and supports the deep truths of other religious traditions.

Jesus of Nazareth

Jesus of Nazareth is the historical medium of Christian faith in God. Some estimate that he was born in 6 BCE and died at the time of Passover in Jerusalem in the year 30 CE. The main sources for knowing about him and his ministry are the Gospels, but a historically accurate portrait cannot be drawn off the surface of the texts. They were put together between forty to seventy years after his death from stories that were constructed from memory of his short ministry of between one to three years. While the Gospels do not always portray what actually happened in historical detail, they provide a substantial portrait of what he did and stood for.

Reconstructing Jesus's teaching and actions is no easy task, and it remains subject to different interpretations. The context combines Jewish memory of release from Egyptian captivity and Babylonian slavery through the power of God and the conflicted reactions to the first-century occupation and taxation under Roman rule. Tensions and expectations were in the air. Moreover, the way the Gospels were put together by writers or editors was intrinsically complicated. On the one hand, the events generated the memories. On the other hand, the writers were people who had faith in Jesus as God's revealer, and their beliefs, developed over decades, helped in writing the history. The Jewish scriptures also aided understanding of what went on in Jesus's ministry. Did Jesus know Isaiah and assume the role of announcing the rule of God? Or did the community, after his death, express their faith in him after the fact as fulfilling that role? Did anything happen exactly as told? No theory of the composition of history or the interpretation of historical texts can be imposed on the Gospels as a whole; each biblical scholar must sort out the evidence presented by each story.[1]

What difference do interpretative differences make? On several issues they may not make a difference that ultimately matters. The faith commitment to the revelation remains foundational, but understanding how Jesus's revelation and the followers' faith came about may differ considerably. One difference that matters should be stated. The medium for Christian faith is not the Bible and not the New Testament text. The text bears witness to Jesus as the anointed Messiah or Christ. That link to the figure in history works subtly as an anchor within the tides of different interpretations.

One cannot really narrate Jesus's ministry chronologically because the ensemble of stories across the Gospels does not have a unifying timeline. This synopsis of Jesus's ministry touches upon his teaching; his actions, such as healing; his prophetic message about the rule of God; and concludes with some facts about his death. The history of Jesus's ministry, however, is just the beginning of the larger story.

---

[1] Marcus J. Borg and N. T. Wright enter into dialogue on these matters. The two authors are highly qualified exegetes who take significantly different positions on these matters, but, as mutually respectful friends, they explain how and why they agree on many things but differ on others. See Marcus J. Borg and N. T. Wright, *The Meaning of Jesus: Two Visions* (San Francisco: HarperSanFrancisco, 2000), 3–27.

Teacher, Healer, and Prophet

The fundamental context for understanding Jesus of Nazareth is first-century Jewish Palestine. Instead of contrasting Jesus with his Jewishness, the whole New Testament appeals to his tradition in order to explain him. The three large categories of teacher, healer, and prophet help because they provide types of figures of his time that offer insights into the individual. As genre is to writing, so public persona is to the form the message takes: it provides an aperture for seeing meaning. Jesus embodied features from all three types of public figures. The Gospels portray Jesus as a teacher, with a band of followers, who moved from village to village with commentary on scripture, short stories or parables, anecdotes, and sayings that were remembered. He was also a faith healer, sometimes putting his hands on people, always appealing to their faith as the deeper medium of cure. Common convictions in the power of spirits framed his healings as exorcisms. These two functions are portrayed as a full day's work in Mark 1:21–39.

While no single persona or portrait of Jesus can exclude the others, the idea that Jesus was a prophet offers an integrating principle and motivation of his ministry. Although prophets are complex figures, the prophetic character of Jesus shows itself principally in the role that *the rule of God* played in all aspects of his ministry. Using the word *rule* rather than *kingdom* of God shifts the meaning to an emphasis on imagining how the world would be, if God's will were being done "on earth as it is heaven" (Mt 6:10). The rule of God is God ruling the lives of people. The model for this idea may have been a symbiosis of the godly king reflecting God's concern for all within the community. Or it may recall the will of God reflected in Torah, not of lawyerly concern for detail but of the creator's concern for the flourishing of all in society that was sealed in a covenantal compact. Giving prophetic scrutiny a "centering" role in Jesus's ministry leads to the idea that the rule of God allowed Jesus to recognize the negativities in religious and social life and to expose them. In many ways, understanding Jesus as an agent of the hoped-for rule of God is a way of describing what is displayed in so many different ways in the gospel stories. Teaching and healing were not add-ons to Jesus's prophetic role but ways of his promoting and participating in God's rule.

Was Jesus conscious of being the Messiah or the final prophet? It is impossible to answer this question historically. One cannot get inside Jesus's intimate consciousness. Simply deciding what level or kind of consciousness would be involved makes the question purely speculative. Those who critically entertain the possibility think in the indirect terms of Jesus's participation in God's will for the world.

Jesus's Representation of God

Reading the Gospels with a realistic desire to capture the events and their significance for life today requires critical attention. Jesus represented God in a variety of ways. One finds a number of simple declarative sayings attributed to Jesus that pronounce that God alone is good; that God loves the world and human beings; that God is a God of life; that God is Father. Jesus also taught through parables, short stories that acted as similes or metaphors for God. God is a betrayed father who heaps blessings on the offending son who returns in ruin; God's rule affronts human justice by paying workers hired late in the day a full wage. Jesus taught with symbolic actions that struck home and had consequences; they showed that God's ways are not human ways. Jesus's demonstration against practices in the temple precincts got people's attention; so did his associations with people branded as public sinners. Some of Jesus's foundational ethical principles that were connected with the rule of God seemed impossible. For example, Jesus taught his fellow Jews to behave like a Samaritan in selfless love of a Jewish enemy as if he were a neighbor. Jesus taught followers how to pray in the Jewish way; that is, praise and exalt God, and then ask God for all the things needed to live authentically, from food to forgiveness.

One can sum up Jesus's teaching as it appears in the witness to his ministry with basic qualities that correspond closely with the tradition of the Jewish scriptures. God is transcendent in spite of the anthropomorphic language: God is God. But God loves God's creation and human beings in it with the fierce love of a parent. God is thus personal and present to all that is. God is savior, of all, but with a special historical bond to Israel. Jesus acts with the saving power that has its source in God's Spirit presence. Jesus's representation of God carefully combines a particular and a large universal or social perspective on God's relation to the world. God intimately relates to each individual, and God is concerned with the character of social relationships that tilt toward certain groups or individuals that are victims and cannot help themselves. Jesus portrays God as the foundation of justice. Jesus's God judges and rules against any social practice that dehumanizes God's people, including individuals like Lazarus, who was simply neglected as he wasted away.

Another way of conceiving Jesus's ministry of representing God and God's rule is formulated in the idea that Jesus himself was a parable of God. The full narrative story of his ministry, of which we have only a fragmentary witness, holistically mediates God's presence. Jesus's person and ministry were a metaphor and symbol of God. When someone asks, "What is God like?" the Christian responds "God is like Jesus."[2] This means that when transcendent reality for which there are no words and no name presents itself to the human imagination, the Christian allows the teaching and action, and ultimately the person embodying them, to represent the character of the still transcendent and unnameable Presence.

Jesus's Death and the Significance of His Humanity

From a historical perspective Jesus's death was as terrible as can be imagined. He paid for his teaching by being accused and then executed by a Roman style of public crucifixion, most probably for political reasons on the part of Roman rule and religious politics on the side of temple leaders. This was hardly the expected fate of messiahs. His death not only shows in a radical way that Jesus was a human being, but it also implicitly identifies him with the massive segment of oppressed humanity that suffers innocently. It compounded the confusion of his followers; his ministry ended in

---

[2] See Juan Luis Segundo, *The Christ of the Ignatian Exercises* (Maryknoll, NY: Orbis Books, 1987), 40; Borg and Wright, *The Meaning of Jesus*, 150, 152.

a disaster that appeared to contradict his whole message of a faithful God of love.

Two reflections might be drawn from this dreadful historical climax of Jesus's ministry. The first is that Jesus's being a human being is a given in constructive christological thinking. The church will develop a teaching that Jesus was divine, but that teaching cannot compete with or challenge Jesus being a human person. In whatever way divinity is predicated of Jesus, it must at the same time be found within his humanity and protect Jesus's being a human being like everyone else (Heb 4:15). Also, the later interpretations of Jesus's death as a divine drama planned in heaven that put a mythological spin on the religious scandal of Jesus's political execution must be rejected on the basis of history.

The second reflection builds on the principle underlying the first. Jesus being a historical human being gives his story universal relevance. The historicity, situatedness, and concreteness of his teaching and his fate are what make Jesus a human being to whom all other human beings can relate. This will have to be recalled again when the formal christological question of Jesus's divinity is broached.

Jesus's Resurrection

The resurrection of Jesus plays an important part in the Christian story. Paul wrote that "if Christ has not been raised, then our preaching is in vain and your faith is in vain" (1 Cor 15:14). Coming to an awareness of Jesus's resurrection was a turning point that enabled the Jesus movement to continue and develop as it did. In terms of a contrast experience, resurrection became part of the positive salutary dimension of the Jesus event itself after his crucifixion.[3]

Theology has the task of critically interpreting how the disciples came to the recognition that Jesus was raised and the logic of the belief. What was and is the evidence for the momentous claim that

---

[3] In this account resurrection refers to what happened to Jesus at his death. Easter experience refers to how the disciples came to the realization that Jesus was alive and risen.

the dead Jesus is alive, and what is its significance? The gospel stories contain no eyewitnesses to the resurrection, that is, to Jesus being raised. The stories give us disciples who came to his tomb to find it empty; angels communicate his resurrection. The main evidence for the resurrection comes in the form of witnesses to Jesus's appearances that bear certain otherworldly qualities: Jesus appears in flesh and blood but is not recognized; the risen Jesus passes through locked doors; his physical presence has a thin, spiritualized character. The variety of appearances and the different kinds of personal and group encounters make it difficult to hypothesize what lay behind the textual testimony.

One can negotiate much of the confusing scriptural data by answering two main questions. The first is what exactly the term *resurrection* refers to and means. All Christians know the answer to this question on a basic level, but a reflective refinement opens up other lines of thinking. The second question is how the followers of Jesus came to the awareness that Jesus was risen. There was a time after Jesus's death when the disciples were scattered and discouraged, and a time when they were spirited witnesses to Jesus alive. An Easter experience refers to how the disciples became aware that Jesus is risen and alive with God. The simple explanation of empirical apparitions may not be plausible for many people today. Theology should try to explain an Easter experience of the first disciples in such a way that it can be recognized as analogous to the consciousness of a Christian believer in today's culture.

The Meaning of Resurrection

The idea of resurrection is based on an image of someone getting up again after being down. Visually, someone asleep resurrects each morning to continue a conscious routine. But, in this case, it refers to coming back to life after being dead. In other words, Jesus was really dead and his body laid to rest for some time. Belief in resurrection was not uncommon in Jesus's time, but it generally referred to something that would occur to many at the end of time. To say that Jesus was resurrected was an astonishing claim, and more has to be said about its character.

What the Gospels refer to with the idea that Jesus is risen needs to be put into sharper focus. For example, commentators on the text generally rule out what may be imagined as a resuscitation of a corpse. Jesus's dead body did not metamorphize back into the living person he had been. The Gospels clearly portray the resurrected Jesus as otherworldly rather than as his former self. Unfortunately, the human imagination tends to imagine Jesus as he was even though the texts indicate something else.

At the same time the Gospels also clearly and insistently affirm that Jesus, the person, had been raised from death and that he was alive. He did not cease to exist as a person. A somewhat prevalent existentialist theology affirms that Jesus's resurrection may be explained by his living on in the memory and lives of his followers. But that theology explains Jesus's resurrection by explaining it away. It is no longer real in the sense of an actual resurrection; the realism of the metaphor has actually been dismissed, and what still exists is not Jesus but his memory as entertained by his followers. Relative to the text, then, this interpretation is mere contrivance.

A simpler and realist interpretation of Jesus's resurrection says that the person Jesus was received into God's life; it really happened, but it was a transcendent "event" or reality. Jesus died into the transcendent power of the God of life; Jesus lives in God on the other side of death. In other words, the life and death character of the subject matter of this case transpires within the sphere of God creating; resurrection invokes God's continuous creation, analogous to existence versus nonexistence by the power of God. The domain or field of thinking involves being and nonbeing. The transition from death to life pertains to the metaphysical order and precisely not to historical or biological changes. Jesus's resurrection was a real event but not an empirical historical event; it happened within the sphere of God. Resurrection means that God continued to hold Jesus in a post-terrestrial existence after his death.

How Jesus's Resurrection Was Revealed

More has to be said about how the disciples learned about Jesus's resurrection. How does one understand the Easter experience of the disciples that allowed them to rise to the invitation of faith in Jesus resurrected? The ordinary explanation comes from the portrayals of the overt apparition narratives. Jesus appeared to the disciples and proved to them the reality of the resurrection by demonstration, sometimes by showing his wounds and sometimes by physically eating. Sometimes the empty tomb is drawn into this logic as if the absence of a body actually indicated resurrection in the sense of a resuscitated corpse.

But an alternative explanation of the appearance stories is less supernaturalistic and more plausible. Rather than being reports of historical events, the appearance stories were written by those who already believed in Jesus's resurrection and who wanted to communicate that reality to those who were unaware of it or who required the attestation of witnesses. In short, the appearance stories explicitly function as indicators of the realism of the resurrection. Jesus is alive, and these witnesses encountered him. In this view, while the stories may succeed in communicating that Jesus was really risen, they do not supply an explanation of how the disciples arrived at this faith. They express a faith already in place. What then was the historical medium that awakened an Easter experience and faith that Jesus was alive?

A plausible way of approaching this begins with the idea that the conviction that Jesus was raised did not happen all at once but was the fruit of a historical process. The process should not be thought of as the result of a single individual having a particular vision, but more of an awareness that grew within the group of followers over an unknown period of time. The idea rests on a supposition that a group of followers remained intact, met together, perhaps shared meals together as they did when Jesus was alive. Gradually it became clear to them that Jesus was present to them as a living rather than merely a remembered presence, and they recognized him in the breaking of bread together.

While this may seem like a convenient story that is made up for the occasion, it corresponds closely with Luke's historical allegory of the disciples on their way to Emmaus from Jerusalem after the death of Jesus (Lk 24:13–35). Generalizing on the carefully chosen details of the story, the disciples could not help talking about the events that ended Jesus's life. In a mysterious way, Jesus, unrecognized but remembered, joined them as they discussed their earlier hopes and how they collapsed with Jesus's death. But the Jesus-stranger explained to them how things actually corresponded with scriptural signs, and the new understanding moved them greatly. Then, when he joined them for an evening meal, they recognized Jesus present with them in the breaking of the bread even as he disappeared. "It is the intention of this legend to narrate what is essential to the origin and nature of the Christian faith."[4] The story recounts a corporate historical form of an Easter experience, mediated by the assemblies, meals, and discussions of his followers, and gradually internalized by them.

This historical reconstruction of a plausible historical revelation that Jesus is alive with God does not end the discussion. What may have been a revelation to Jesus's followers may not be so obvious to someone in the twenty-first century who participates in a metaphysically skeptical culture. We need a larger generalized theory of the revelation of Jesus's resurrection to bridge the historical witness and a present-day appeal to faith. Is there a theoretical description that can portray what happened to the disappointed disciples and may also happen to people today?

The following four dimensions of an Easter experience describe distinct but open elements that analogously apply to past and current coming to faith in Jesus's resurrection. First, belief in Jesus's resurrection logically entails some knowledge of Jesus. Jesus is part of the subject matter to which faith is directed. The mode of this knowledge differs between a contemporary disciple and one approaching Jesus at a distance today, but the Gospels keep the memory of Jesus alive. Second, as in faith itself, belief in Jesus's resurrection has to spring from a combination of hope and faith surging within the believer. The impulse and motivation have their roots deep within the self. A third dimension of coming to faith in Jesus's resurrection credits the impulse toward it to God as Spirit

---

[4] Hans Dieter Betz, "The Origin and Nature of Christian Faith according to the Emmaus Legend," *Interpretation* 23 (January 1969): 38.

within as an inner witness. Faith is a function of freedom but one may be surprised by a faith that may not be fully in one's control. Fourth, an intellectual move helps to uncover the plausibility of this description of an Easter experience. It entails reading the appearance stories as expressions of the prior faith of the writers rather than as actual historical motives for faith.

The last point represents a large shift for someone who reads scripture in an uncritical way. But if one reads the world with an alert sophisticated and questioning spirit, it will be difficult to accept scriptural narratives at face value. Although this is meant as a general theory, it requires accommodations of the continuous Christian Easter experience to the culture and audience it addresses.

The Divinity of Jesus

Christians believe in the divinity of Jesus. They first accepted Jesus as Messiah, but messiahship did not entail divinity. Belief in some form of Jesus's divinity developed over a long period of time and took more twists and turns than can be communicated in a short space. This section aims mainly at capturing the fluidity and complexity of the historical discussion while noting that it was guided by certain basic principles. The early church developed some classic doctrines that are interpreted differently in various churches and translated into new non-Western languages. Yet these doctrines, as classics, set a framework and enshrine principles that are universally relevant across different Christian traditions.

The four subsections that follow set out large fields of discussion: the idea of Jesus as savior and the salvation he mediates; how the idea that Jesus is a divine figure arose and how it was handled; the doctrine that Jesus embodied two natures, human and divine; and the relation between two distinct frameworks for understanding Jesus Christ. Drawing a conceptual map or setting out a linguistic glossary will be helpful in formulating one's own beliefs about Jesus. The section aims to provide a framework and a few principles for understanding different present-day conceptions of the classic doctrines.

From Salvation to Divinity

The church did not affirm the divinity of Jesus all at once. There is little sign in the Gospels of Mark, Matthew, and Luke that Jesus was considered a strictly divine figure; he never self-identified as Yahweh but related to God as a creature would. It was only three hundred years later, in 325, that Jesus was decisively affirmed as being divine at a general council held in Nicaea. A doctrine arrived at through centuries of debate cannot be obvious; as a declaration it is hemmed in by context, perspective, and discussion.

A basic logic can be found across the arguments for Jesus's divinity that still has merit and thus can be understood as a principle for understanding christological doctrines. In a phrase, the principle says that Jesus was considered divine because he was experienced as savior. The operative insight in this maxim lies in the recognition that the salvation spoken of here involves transcendent authority and ultimacy. Because it cuts close to one's being, it is attributed to transcendent power. The reasons for Jesus's divinity are rooted in various experiences of being saved or liberated at the deep reaches of human existence. From the perspective of the seeker, doctrines do not respond to intellectual curiosity but primarily to a quest for existential liberation that can only come from a transcendent source. Divinity was predicated of Jesus in response to a search for salvation, and Jesus offers a salvation that can only come from God.

An experience of salvation should not be limited by a single formula; the New Testament bears witness to its existential uniqueness in each person. The early Jesus movement understood how Jesus saves in many different ways; Jesus redeems by paying a ransom, frees from slavery, reconciles after division, offers satisfaction for wrongdoing, establishes peace, expiates for sin by being a sin offering, wins forgiveness of sins, sends the Spirit, teaches, justifies, sanctifies, renews the world, promises victory over demonic powers, and offers fullness of life. Salvation occurs whenever people experience God's love, forgiveness, acceptance, or empowerment in their lives. Christian salvation or liberation occurs when Jesus reveals the character of God and makes God present to human lives and reconciles their enmities. These effects derive from being drawn into a relationship with God through the mediation of Jesus, and one's relationship to God creates a bond with other people. Jesus began to be thought of as divine because he mediated the effects of a divine presence. Some simple principle like "one cannot give what one does not have" was operative here.

Paul Tillich penetrated deeply into where the psychoanalytic self becomes a consciousness of oneself in the face of being itself. He found there three forms of anxiety that are indigenous to human existence and threaten human integrity and peace. One is fear of death that stalks human life; it is less the pain than the unknown void that death threatens or leads to. Guilt and a fear of ultimate condemnation provide a second disruption of existence. Will there be an assessment of our moral being? A third gnawing apprehension lies in a perception of emptiness and meaninglessness beneath the surface of life. We pass time and may accomplish many important things, but they seem superficial on the large horizon of time, space, and being itself.[5] These threats to human being thrive in the context of the metaphysical skepticism, relativism, and pessimism that accompany developed societies. Tillich's division acts like a typology to help interpret the many metaphors used by the various communities reflected in the New Testament.

The Doctrine of Jesus's Divinity

The doctrine of Jesus's divinity was finally promulgated in 325 at a general council summoned by Constantine. But it had a historical background that complicated its declarative assertion. During the course of the second century the most prominent language for discussing the divinity of Jesus was drawn from the Prologue of John's Gospel: "In the beginning was the Word, and the Word was with God, and the Word was God. . . . And the Word became flesh and lived among us" (John 1:1, 14). The term *word,* translating the Greek *logos,* had resonance with Greek philosophy and culture. *Logos* symbolized not only God's declared intention, but also the reason

---

[5] Paul Tillich, *The Courage to Be* (New Haven, CT: Yale University Press, 1952), 40–57.

and the intelligence that suffused reality. In Hebrew scriptural culture God's word was God's will, spoken and effective. "God said, 'Let there be light'; and there was light" (Gen 1:4). In short, texts like these provided the framework for discussing Jesus's divinity indirectly in terms of the character of the Word of God incarnate in him.

In the early fourth century in Egypt the strictly divine character of the Word of God was called into question, not for the first time, by a certain Arius, who thus provided the name of the heretical Arianism. Reductively, what he taught was interpreted to maintain that the Word of God, already considered as distinct from God as Father, was created before time and thus had to be considered a creature and not strictly divine. The reaction to this as represented by Athanasius, the champion of what became orthodoxy, was that, if Jesus as Word incarnate was not divine, he could not be savior. Thus the Nicene Creed clearly affirmed that Jesus was divine because the Word he incarnated was strictly divine: of the same nature or being as the Father.

The pros and cons of this doctrine cannot be fully addressed here, but the teaching requires a brief comment. The framework of the debate is highly conceptual and, though not unrelated, distant from the concrete experiences of Christian encounter with the Jesus of the Gospels. The framework of "Word" language virtually ignores the witness of the four Gospels to the role of God as Spirit at work in Jesus and his ministry. But in its favor, the Nicene Creed states clearly that not less than God was at work in Jesus for salvation or ultimate human liberation.

The Doctrine of Two Natures

After the doctrine of Nicaea was in place, another extended discussion, this time focused on the person of Jesus of Nazareth, occupied theologians. Jesus was already characterized as the incarnation of a strictly divine Word of God. How then was one to understand his human status? Was he truly a human being like others during his life on earth? A line of thinking on this question associated with Alexandrian theologians proposed that the phrase "the divine Word took flesh" provided a model for thinking about this question. The

Word of God, construed as distinct from God as Father, took on the physical and biological aspects of flesh and blood. In effect, the Word of God was the operating subject within Jesus; the Word of God assumed the role of the human spirit or soul, the inner life that animated the "flesh." This incarnational or "Word-Flesh" pattern, in the end, did not really preserve an integral humanity. Jesus looked more like a divine subject in human clothing or physical appearance. He is not at all like us interiorly.

Another image, often referred to as an indwelling model, associated with theologians from Syria and specifically Antioch, held on to the idea that Jesus was a historical human being. They thought of the divine Word of God "dwelling within" an integral human person. The critics of this description of the person of Jesus felt that, while it left Jesus's human character intact, it posited an unresolved duality within his person. How did the two "subjects" relate to each other?[6] Which one is the actor? The integral unity of Jesus as a human seemed to be left unexplained. The church needed a formula for transcending and holding together Jesus's humanity and divinity within the integrity of an identity. The response was the formula of a single person with two natures that was formulated at the Council of Chalcedon in 451.[7]

---

[6] This question is similar to the unity of creator and creature discussed in Chapter 5. But it lacks the subtlety of Thomas Aquinas or Bernard of Clairvaux before him. See Bernard of Clairvaux, "On Grace and Free Will," in *Treatises III* (Kalamazoo, MI: Cistercian Publications, 1977), 106.

[7] "Jesus Christ: the same perfect in divinity and perfect in humanity, the same truly God and truly man, of a rational soul and a body; consubstantial with the Father as regards his divinity, and the same consubstantial with us as regards his humanity; like us in all respects except for sin; begotten before the ages from the Father as regards his divinity, and in the last days the same for us and for our salvation from Mary, the virgin God-bearer as regards his humanity; one and the same Christ, Son, Lord, only-begotten, acknowledged in two natures which undergo no confusion, no change, no division, no separation; at no point was the difference between the natures taken away through the union, but rather the property of both natures is preserved and comes together into a single person and a single subsistent being; he is not parted or divided into two persons, but is one and the same only-begotten Son, God, Word, Lord Jesus Christ." The translation is drawn from *Decrees of the Ecumenical Councils*, ed. Norman P. Tanner (Washington, DC: Georgetown University Press, 1990).

This doctrine was a compromise; it is a practical formula with a language that did not explain but held together the values of a single person who had two distinct and unconfused natures. Its value may be seen in its laying down limits that cannot be transgressed: truly human and truly divine. It also combined highly technical language with a commonsensical meaning that was useful: one person, two natures or kinds of being. The formula is minimalistic but clear. The main problem with the formula appears when one takes it as theological explanation and tries to identify what a nature is and who the personal subject Jesus of Nazareth really is. The nature of the divine is transcendent and unknown. It certainly cannot be placed in contrastive parallel with human nature.

Two Scriptural Metaphors for Christology

Exegeting the template provided by the Council of Chalcedon sends Christology down a far too narrow path; it is best understood as a practical doctrine governing limits rather than a positive theory. The New Testament has stronger, more comprehensive, and more meaningful language for constructive Christology today. Two specific metaphors among others provide simpler, equally metaphysical, and accessible language for consideration of Jesus's human and divine character: Word and Spirit.

Both Word and Spirit are metaphors; all such language is metaphorical. They both refer to mediated experiences of God or the effects of God's presence in the world. The things of the world are there because they are the effects of God's declarative will (Word) or because the invisible animating power of God (Spirit) works within. Each metaphorical symbol has its own history and semantic associations within the Hebrew scriptures. Word suggests God's intention, intelligence, wisdom, and power. Spirit suggests God's inner dynamism providing life and animating and energizing power. Each symbol, applied to Jesus, indicates God's presence and activity within him; each accounts for his authority, for his saving activity. Each one, like any name or characteristic predicated of God, requires that its meaning be negated when applied to God, because God transcends all names and language. They share the affirmation that God works within, as invisible Presence and power, yet in a way that recognizes God's transcendence. Both metaphors were personified as agents of the power of God. This is best illustrated by God's Wisdom, which the wisdom literature frequently personifies. But the reification of Word or Spirit, turning scriptural personification into what it is not, an object with an identity, exceeds scriptural usage. It is always better to say "God as Word" and "God as Spirit" than to imagine that scripture is dividing God into persons or distinct elements by terms like *wisdom, word, glory,* or *spirit.* It makes no sense to think that the Word of God is anything else than God as metaphorical Word or that the Spirit of God is anything else than God experienced as invisible power. Christology best takes the lead of either a Spirit Christology or a Word Christology from the New Testament; to do both together seems somewhat redundant. Each says what Nicaea affirmed: no less than God was at work in Jesus mediating human salvation or liberation.

Jesus's Divinity Reclaimed

The theological affirmation of the divinity of Jesus Christ consoles many and confounds others. Before turning to constructive reflections on the meaningfulness of Jesus's divinity, one has to be clear that some naive understandings of this doctrine are misleading. Some conceptions of Jesus's divinity merit spontaneous reactions against them. What does the divinity of Jesus *not* mean?

The divinity of Jesus cannot mean that Jesus was simply God in the appearance of a human being. This broad idea in varying degrees is often reflected in the pattern of incarnation, where the inner subject of Jesus of Nazareth is really the divine Word, which Nicaea affirmed was not less the Godhead than the creator God, or Yahweh, or the Father. Many of the texts of the theologians of the early church refer to the subjectivity of Jesus as the "intelligence" and the "will" of the divine Word. For one who is not attentive, the doctrine seems to encourage the imagination spontaneously to regard the subject, Jesus, as though he were not a human self or being, but rather God within a human physicality. The desire to learn about how Jesus appeared to his contemporaries has mediated a historicist realism that rejects as mythological a Jesus who is really God in a human guise. The language of John's Prologue, "the Word was made flesh," does not represent the order of human encounter and understanding that begins with history. Christianity requires a plainer and subtler way of expressing the true divinity of Jesus in a plausible way. It begins with taking Jesus as all know him to be: a human being. Only then does the theological problem become evident: how can we predicate divinity of a human being? What follows are a few principles that do not resolve the mystery of the incarnation but help to guide thinking about it.

A first reflection drawn from previous chapters appeals to the mystery of God. Karl Rahner expressed this in the clearest terms: God is absolute incomprehensible mystery. Although Christians accept Jesus of Nazareth as a distinctive revelation of God, this does not mean that God ceases to be intrinsically beyond human understanding. God being incarnate in Jesus does not make God sensibly perceptible or empirically available. God remains a mysterious reality in Jesus; it can be communicated only to faith by a resonant consciousness of God within the self. The whole process of manifestation, communication, and faithful recognition transpires in the sphere of religious consciousness that is mediated through the overt objective mediation of Jesus's ministry.

The recognition of the divinity of Jesus has to be understood as a process of coming to a faith awareness. To affirm that Jesus is divine means that one has encountered God in or through him. The gospel stories show Jesus's attachment to God or, reciprocally, God's hold on Jesus's consciousness. His human reactions constitute his manifestation of God's power; he reveals God through his actions and God's intentions through his teaching. The affirmation of Jesus's divinity has to be rooted in the dynamics of revelation and faith. A person becomes aware that Jesus bears the power of the immanence of God, when the same person recognizes God within his or her self, ratifying the absolute value of human existence itself. The affirmation that Jesus is somehow divine entails Jesus as a human being who communicates the immanence of God in the world and is thus the basis for the value of existence itself.

Jesus's divinity consists of his union with God because of God's being immanent within him. The portrayal of the intimate and conjunct action of creator and creature in Chapter 5 provides a metaphysical model. Since Jesus is a human being, his divinity manifests the potential for union with God of everyone, of all of humanity. Jesus is human existence united with God because God is immanent to human existence. The more Jesus of Nazareth is turned into God rather than being a human being empowered by God, the more the point of "incarnation" and God's presence to the rest of creation and human existence is undermined. A basic maxim of patristic theology applies to this case: if Jesus is not one of us, then we are not saved. Jesus is a revelation of what finite human existence is and can be: conscious response to the intrinsic dependence of creation on God. Jesus is God's presence become intentional in an intense and exemplary way. Jesus's divinity is the immanence of God to finitude, to human existence, and to each person as an individual.

Jesus's divinity does not compete with the divine immanence that holds all reality in existence. One might say with Edward Schillebeeckx that it consists of a more intense or concentrated presence and power of God. But one cannot say that the immanence of God in Jesus is different in kind than God's presence to other human beings. To do so would precisely rob the incarnation of its intrinsic significance as was just said: God's incarnation in Jesus is the creator's incarnation in all created reality. The point of Jesus's salvific revelation is precisely its universal relevance. Jesus mediates human reconciliation not by being exclusive but by manifesting God's validating presence within all people. The liberation mediated by Jesus consists of God's openness to religious pluralism, to overcoming religious animosity due to competitiveness. Jesus affirms the immanence of ultimate reality and its non-dual presence to the world, making the whole of it a sacred place and a sacred enterprise.

Finally, it is important to distinguish the religious and the moral response to Jesus and the immanent divinity he manifests, and only then to recognize their inseparability. Jesus primarily mediates God's presence and God's benevolent character. This awakens in a pointed way an absolute dependence on God and a God-consciousness that should bathe all human response to reality with a primal sense of gratitude. The moral sensibility of a Christian is rooted in the religious; the spiritual relationship with God suffuses Christian morality. Preaching that moves directly from Jesus to specific moral actions dangerously misrepresents God by reducing God to a lawgiver or, worse, a cop. The religious sphere is vastly deeper and more comprehensive than the moral order. To say that Jesus is divine means that the power of the creator God shines forth in his ministry and encompasses all reality. This includes and gives a rationale for moral behavior. Moreover, recognizing other manifestations of the transcendent grounding of human existence does not minimize Jesus's divinity. Rather Jesus's ministry and person show in a relatively clear way that the divine presence and power found in him are prevalent generally in the world. St. Paul adds that God's presence and power only appear as "through a glass darkly" (1 Cor 13:12). And David Tracy notices that God's immanence can only be found in fragments; but such revelations can be encountered, and they are fragments of something real.

This account of the historical development, logic, and content of Christology travels further than the space warrants. It offers no more than an outline for discussion. The positions taken on delicate matters of doctrine represent opinions within a wider conversation addressing different audiences. It will achieve its purpose in this introduction to Christian theology if it provokes interest and conversation rather than simple assent. The point of Christology, as Schubert Ogden insisted, remains Christ's mediation of human liberation in standing before God.

7

God as Spirit

This chapter returns to the cultural feeling of pessimism in the face of so much human suffering and the sheer inability of the human species to deal with it. Human beings can solve problems up to a point. But many spheres of human degradation exceed the human capacity to manage them. They are too entrenched to master: extended poverty, hunger, racism, and interminable war. In today's world these are not abstractions; the bodies pile up and are discarded. Human beings find ways of dealing with the pervasive negative situation. Individuals and groups can choose to ignore the problems or block them out by psychic compartmentalization. Or people can make some kind of peace with the inevitabilities of the human condition. Some stake out a narrower sphere of personal and social space and find fulfillment in it. But these avoidance mechanisms may harbor a larger unfocused feeling of helplessness, or a cynicism reconciled to cosmic injustice, and thus a quiet but debilitating pessimism. The damaged human condition remains the wider and implicitly negative field for individual or group pursuit of personal happiness within a narrowed purview.

Chapter 4 dealt with theology as a discipline in the face of evil. It showed how a religious consciousness and a faith relationship with God intrinsically included a distinctly moral response to the world, especially to other human beings. Using the logic of a negative experience of contrast, it considered how theology seeks to understand the divine source of salvation from dehumanizing forces. Theology becomes a practical social academic discipline when it moves the religious imagination to react against negative situations and seek liberation.

This chapter also addresses cosmic pessimism, but it shifts the focus of the discussion to the sphere of personal spirituality. The social and the individual aspects of life cannot be separated from each other, but the distinction allows one to ask the question, "How does Christianity give meaning to my life?" To personalize a question means to examine how the various dimensions of an issue are worked out in the lives of individual persons. What are the experiences of salvation and liberation when individual persons internalize and act out the faith and beliefs of Christianity? Can an internalization of the message about God mediated by Jesus overcome the subtle forces of cosmic pessimism in the personal lives of believers? These personal questions open up the possibilities of corporate Christian spirituality.

The chapter approaches these questions by entering the theological domain of God as Spirit and the Spirit's operation in the Christian life. A first definition of the meaning of "God as Spirit" describes it as referring to the source of effects attributed to God present and working within the world. This could refer to God experienced in one's own life or to manifestations of the power of God within the external world. The "Spirit of God" is an important category across both Testaments of the Bible, and it functions as the central controlling metaphor for God in this chapter.

Several major theologians across the history of Christian thought staked out markers for understanding how the Spirit of God functions in the world. For example, a primary reference for the term *grace,* which characterizes the foundational positive relationship of God to human beings as forgiveness and love, is God as Spirit present and active within a person. Here grace refers to God's love and forgiveness experienced as operating within human beings. God as Spirit and grace become synonymously God's presence and action of loving acceptance. As such, grace sets up the principal category for developing a Christian anthropology, that is, an understanding of human existence as it stands as creature before God. The theology of grace, of human beings living within the sphere of God's loving presence, thus constituted a framework for the discussion of how human beings in turn should relate to God and one another. In short, *God's grace* became a standard term in Christian theology that described how God as Spirit is present and active within human beings. As a result, the understandings of God as Spirit and synonymously of the operation of God's grace became the deep structure for the Christian understanding of how human beings should respond to God and direct their lives.

Given this framework, the chapter will first look at the idea of God as Spirit in scripture to set up the root metaphor for God acting in the world. It will also consider how major theologians such as Augustine, Aquinas, John Calvin, Friedrich Schleiermacher, and Karl Rahner understood God's relationship toward human beings using the categories of Holy Spirit and grace. The second part of the chapter turns to how Christians are called to lead their lives in response to the Spirit or God's grace. The section bears the title "Christian Spirituality," because the way people live defines them and their relationship with God. So the question arises: to what does God as Spirit summon human freedom? The responses to these questions will draw upon the teachings of Jesus preserved in the Gospels and the interpretations of them in the rest of the New Testament. They will show the reciprocity between the Christian life described in this chapter and the way liberation theologies described it in Chapter 4. The third part will discuss eschatology or the end of time. It will show how resurrection holds out the possibility of absolute eternal meaning for the life of each person, for the species, and for the world. That absolute future turns spirituality into dedication to the human project within the world. Thus does the final section sum up Christian life in terms of "resistance, creativity, and hope."

The Idea of God as Spirit

Spirit in scripture is a primal metaphor representing God's presence and activity in the world. Spirit refers broadly to unseen power or force. The wind remains invisible, but the movement of the trees shows its presence and the degree of its intensity. The idea of spirit seems to protect God's transcendence by making a distinction between God and the effects of God's presence in the world. But that does not work: God is where God acts. Like the wind, because it lacks a bodily or physical presence to the eye, God as Spirit can only be visually perceived through its effects. The point here is missed by noting the materiality of the breath or wind. The metaphor works by allowing the lack of direct visibility and hardened resistance to touch to suggest other ways of detecting the presence and power of a transcendent force surrounding the situation and at work within the world. Science knows full well that the wind is a form of matter, and this demonstrates how religious language aligns more easily with aesthetic perception. Thinking of God as Spirit rules out the possibility of direct empirical evidence of God and attunes the imagination to other forms of perception.

More accessible than the Spirit of God in itself, for that remains inscrutable, the signs and the effects of the presence and power of God lay scattered across the texts of the Bible. The examples are many. The Spirit is God's actual power of creation: "The Spirit of God was moving over the face of the waters" (Gen 1:2). The Spirit of God is the Spirit of life as breath in the lungs. God said through Ezekiel, "I will put my Spirit within you, and you shall live" (Ezek 37:14). Life here connotes various levels of vitality. The Spirit of God empowers leaders. When the people of Israel called upon God for help, "the Spirit of the Lord came upon" the one chosen to lead (Judg 3:10). The Spirit of God inspires. Moses testified to one so singled out: God "has filled him with the divine Spirit [of God], with skill, intelligence, and knowledge in every kind of craft" (Ex 35:31). Isaiah the prophet famously wrote,

> The Spirit of the Lord God is upon me,
>   because the LORD has anointed me;
> he has sent me to bring good news to the oppressed,

and it enabled him to perform healing actions (Isa 61:1). Luke portrayed Jesus appropriating Isaiah's words (Lk 4:21) at some time after his baptism when "the Holy Spirit descended upon him" (Lk 3:22). The Spirit of God accounts for charismatic leadership and capacities to be an agent of God's ways in the world.

In sum, the meaning of God as Spirit really correlates with ways in which people encounter God in the world or in their lives. It points to God "within" the world. The term provided biblical language and sources for reflecting on questions about the dynamics of spiritual life and God at work within persons as found in the theological tradition.

Western Theological Tradition

The theology of God as Spirit developed along two main tracks in Western Christianity: one speculated on the nature of God as Spirit as part of God as Trinity. There the word *Trinity* practically became a synonym for God, and the Holy Spirit was one of the triad. The other track considered how the Holy Spirit operated within human life and, with Augustine, became associated with the theology of grace. As just noted, grace refers to God's love and forgiveness of humankind, and Augustine associated the working of God's grace with the Holy Spirit. After Augustine, theology maintained a close alliance between God as Spirit and God operating in human freedom drawing a saving response of human beings to God from within.

Five theologians represent theological appropriations of the role of the Spirit of God in Christian life in a profound, lasting, and fruitful way. All have distinct contexts and sets of problems to which they are responding. But within the local character of their constructions, one can retrieve classic concepts that can be drawn forward and appropriated in a present-day context. All of these theologians focus on the Spirit of God as it works within human subjectivity: God as Spirit is an interior presence, influence, and empowering energy within the human person. The mode of perception may be dwelt upon, as in a phenomenology of a conversion experience, but that is not the main point. The emphasis lies in the recognition that divine presence and help works within each person through the mechanisms of faith that underlie the daily operations of life.[1] A Christian view of the human person, anthropology, includes the idea that God is present to all people and can be recognized within them.

Augustine's theology of grace, in fact, did not hold that God's grace was operative in all people; it was limited by a strong conception of the power of sin over human freedom. But his description of how grace actually worked, his witness, bears the signs of experience. When he asked, why is there goodness at all in the world? his response appealed to "divine help," which was grace and was the presence and action of the Spirit of God. God's Spirit broke open a human spirit trapped inside itself; it gave the human spirit new eyes to see value outside the self and the human will a power to transcend the self curved in on itself. He used spatial imagery: the human spirit is imprisoned by the weight of matter; the Holy Spirit gives the human spirit the power to appreciate higher altruistic values and soar. From Augustine we learn that an inner power of self-transcendence in human life reflects an invitation from God as Spirit.

Thomas Aquinas's theology of grace translates the scriptural witness to the divine Spirit into a complex Aristotelian language of how substantial change occurs in physical beings, that is, how something can become a new kind of being. What does Paul mean when he says, "If anyone is in Christ, he is a new creation; the old has passed away, behold, the new has come" (2 Cor 5:17)? Aquinas responds to this with an idea that grace bestows on us what amounts to a new nature. Prescinding from his technical construction, one can still offer a few comments about how his moves represent a powerful conception of the working of grace.

God can be perceived as present to a human being in two ways: anonymously as creator, and personally as an accepted power in one's life by faith. The second mode of presence, which Aquinas calls grace, sets up a transformed inner disposition of a person. When faith accepts the Spirit of God into people's lives, their intelligence and

---

[1] It should be clear that Christian doctrine holds that the divine Spirit is not less than God; it is God as Spirit. This means that God as Spirit is God creating and being present to creation as its inner sustaining ground. God as Spirit is thus present to all creation, but able to be recognized in humans as beings reflectively conscious of their own being.

will begin to work with the new transcendent powers of faith, hope, and love. These new powers, in turn, enable persons to operate on a new level of moving toward their final destiny of personal union with God. Aquinas concentrated on the effects of the Spirit within a human life. He thought of God as Spirit elevating persons with new spiritual motivation, enabling them to act within an expanded horizon and to live for a higher goal. He proposes a metaphysical framework for thinking, but it easily translates into a description of psychological conviction and motivation. This is what his theology of grace means by becoming a new creature: living on a higher plane toward final union with God.

John Calvin was also firmly convinced that the Holy Spirit operated in the foundations of a Christian life of faith. Like Augustine, he recognized the power of sin, and he emphasized that there could be no faith without the operation of God as Spirit working within a person. He was moved by the text of Romans: "God's love has been poured into our hearts through the Holy Spirit that has been given to us" (Rom 5:5). Calvin was Christocentric; Christ is savior, the external teacher who instructs. But the Holy Spirit operates within a person and accounts for human reception. The Holy Spirit is the inner teacher "by whose effort the promise of salvation penetrates into our minds, a promise that would otherwise only strike the air or beat upon our ears."[2] Calvin reminds us that external tradition of Christian life in community, everything historical and objective, also has a dimension of interiority, where revelation comes alive in experience and personal life. His theology of the Spirit transforms the externals of Christian faith life into a personalist key. Calvin makes Christian life into a constant dialogue with God as Spirit.

Friedrich Schleiermacher describes the work of God as Spirit pointedly in his description of the church. As he defines it, the Spirit of God refers to the power of God within creatures. The effects of

---

[2] John Calvin, *Institutes of the Christian Religion*, ed. John T. McNeill (Philadelphia: Westminster Press, 1950), 3.1.4; "Indeed, the Word of God is like the sun, shining upon all those to whom it is proclaimed, but with no effect among the blind. Now, all of us are blind by nature in this respect. Accordingly, it cannot penetrate into our minds unless the Spirit, as the inner teacher, through his illumination makes entry for it" (3.2.34).

that power become conscious in the person of faith and the member of the church. As in Augustine, faith is the consciousness of being dependent on God, and this becomes an actual influence on individual persons and the whole community that is the church. As in Calvin, the effects of God's being present to persons move them away from the power of sin and toward eternal meaning and truth. The Spirit of God is a force of attraction and unity within the church community. It militates against division, enmity, and separation. Fragmentation within the church, and hostility and antagonism within communities of various sizes, go against the fundamental dynamism of the Spirit of God. The realism of Schleiermacher's sense of being absolutely dependent on God's presence unites his doctrines of creation and of the Spirit of God, and together they make his theology of the Spirit foundational relative to the church and personal spiritual life.

Karl Rahner helps to bring post-Enlightenment relevance to the working of the Holy Spirit through his theology of grace. His major contribution to Christian theology is grounded in an insight that his theological construction sought to validate. He realized that the Western tradition since Augustine presupposed that the gratuity of grace and the serendipitous effectiveness of the Holy Spirit in human lives correlated with scarcity. He understood that something could be offered to all and still be a pure gift. He could not conceive of God failing actively to love what, after all, God created. Whether or not people accepted it, or in whatever way they accepted it, God's grace or the Holy Spirit's presence as an offer of love was present to all people from their first moment of existence. Creation and grace, or the offer of God's presence, love, and forgiveness, are always simultaneously entwined. One can expand Rahner's insight and maintain that grace, God as Spirit, and God's love and forgiveness are identical. Perhaps the language indicates different perspectives. But, at the very least, creation and grace mutually imply each other. They are inseparable. More about that in what follows.

Later Developments in the Theology of God as Spirit

The second half of the twentieth century has witnessed a number of developments in the Christian theology of the Western world.

They have been encouraged by the expanded horizon of thinking that has been negotiated by global communications and trade; increased travel and the interdependence of nations; cosmopolitan cities; and an explosive new picture of the universe, the earth, and the development of the human species. These developments have occasioned increased questioning of traditional theological conceptions and promoted adjustments to make them more intelligible in a new intellectual culture. Four developments in the practical theology of the Holy Spirit today differentiate it from the tradition.

First of all, the theological description of the functioning of God as Spirit sounds very much like the description of ongoing or "concurrent" creation. God did not create in the past and stop; God is continually creating. The two concepts have different immediate symbolic and linguistic sources. But it would be difficult to imagine that they were not referring to the same subject matter. The effect of God creating is finite reality, and God's creating puts God's active presence within what is being created. The primal metaphor of the Spirit of God signifies God's presence in the world that God is creating. The character of the Spirit of God, however, transcends an objective power and is interwoven with the favor and blessing of a personal God. While existing itself is blessing, the Spirit of God comes to consciousness as gift and communicates a new authorizing power of being. The scriptural witness to the gifts of the Spirit have their analogues in present-day experience. Once God as creator is recognized as personal, the qualities of grace may be folded back into a conception of God creating. The imagination does not have to force the merging of God as gracious Spirit with God creating; each concept positively reinforces the other.

Second, more can be said about the non-reductive merger of the ideas of God as Spirit and continual creation. The dialogue with science has forced theology to take another look at the interventionist character of the language describing the work of the Spirit. This is obviously true relative to the primal language of scripture, where God is constantly intervening in Israel's history, winning battles for them, and actively guiding human history. Science, by contrast, can find no evidence of God intervening into the flow of natural processes. Science reasons on the premise of naturalism and has had compelling success in shaping humanity's view of the world. The catalyst of science, moreover, has helped to clarify some basic theological ideas. If God as creating Spirit is always present in the world all the time, there is no need of God intervening. If God's immanent presence is transcendent, there can be no question of empirical evidence of God's immanence; it intrinsically transcends overt manifestation. God as active agent simply suffuses all of reality as a *divine* presence rather than a force that can be detected by modes of empirical measurement.

Third, the idea of God as Spirit as a resident Spirit rather than an intervening Spirit has a scriptural foundation and significant pastoral consequences. The term *Shekinah* is less a biblical concept than a commentary on the idea that God's presence is frequently described as dwelling in a place. In many respects, *Shekinah* is a synonym for God as Spirit, but it connotes attachment to a special place: God dwells in the tabernacle that Moses built in the desert (Ex 40:34); God dwelt in the Temple in Jerusalem; God dwelt in God's people. *Shekinah* is thus God as Spirit, but less interventionist and more an abiding presence.[3] If God as Spirit is conceived as interventionist, one will be disappointed when a crisis occurs and God does not show up. But if one understands that God is already there, an abiding Presence, one can still have faith and hope because an obvious contradiction has been resolved. Recall how Emil Fackenheim responded to the question of how Jewish faith could preserve the root experiences of God being involved in Jewish history in the face of the catastrophe of the Holocaust. He pointed to the idea of *Shekinah* or God's being present to the Jewish people and accompanying them. Whatever happened to them, even in the death camps, God was with them in their innocent suffering.[4]

Finally, the symbol "God as Spirit" correlates with the immanent presence of God to the reality that God is always creating and sustaining. This identity overcomes a contradiction that is common

---

[3] Roger Haight, *Faith and Evolution: A Grace-Filled Naturalism* (Maryknoll, NY: Orbis Books, 2019), 98–99.

[4] Emil L. Fackenheim, *God's Presence in History: Jewish Affirmations and Philosophical Reflections* (New York: Harper Torchbooks, 1972), 25–30.

and even widespread. It imagines that there is some tension between God as Spirit or as grace and a natural world. The idea of a contrast here overflows into a competitive relationship between God's action in the world and human freedom. This opposition suffuses Western Christian thought, if not overtly, as a tacit anthropomorphic presupposition in discussions of human agency and God's action. An implicit dualism of competing agents shows up consistently in conceptions of grace and freedom. Synergism is negative because the framework proposes that human freedom can somehow earn salvation or that the working of God is displacing nature or free human agency. This rivalry is absolutely foreign to the idea of creation. God as the power of being categorically transcends finite agency. God as Spirit operates as an entirely different kind of presence and agency. From the beginning, in the very process of sustaining reality, God as gracious Spirit creates, sustains, and energizes human freedom. The implicit supposition of a zero-sum competition subverts the basic Christian vision of the gracious creating Spirit of God.

A more coherent picture of the world may be called a grace-filled naturalism and a Spirit-filled world. This idea does not compete with a salutary secularization but fills time, space, and matter with the positive creating Spirit of God.

Christian Spirituality

Scriptural and doctrinal ideas bear meaning when they correlate with experience and prevailing consciousness. An examination of scriptural ideas and the theological interpretations that make up the history of Christian thought can remain on an objective hermeneutical level. But the question of how grace affects present-day experience shifts attention from objective history to an existential sphere. The topic of spirituality transposes the idea of God as Spirit into the subjective sphere of experience where it can resonate in personal and social life.

The theology of God as Spirit, especially where it takes the practical form of a theology of grace in the theological tradition, describes the structure of the relationship between God and human beings. It draws creation theology and the liberation mediated by Jesus Christ into the existential relationship that governs Christian life. In other words, the theology of Spirit and grace deals with ideas that imagine and express the ways in which God deals with human beings and human persons respond to God. The questions that underlie Christian spirituality address the functional relationships or exchanges that constitute Christian living. The basic issue takes the form of how human beings are united with God in the course of living their lives.

On this premise, the term *spirituality* in this compact presentation refers to the way Christians lead their lives in relationship with the God revealed in Jesus Christ. This interpretation resists a reduction of spirituality to explicitly religious practices and incorporates the whole of one's life into the relationship with God. The far greater part of most people's lives consists of work, play, and various social engagements. These have to have spiritual value and cannot be left out of the calculus of a person's relation to God. Spirituality draws upon the maxim that one's actions better represent one's inner intentionality than do words or formulas. This does not drive a wedge between thought and action, between religious practices and secular life, but weds them together as dimensions of a more encompassing formula. Spirituality as a comprehensive disposition that includes all human behavior disallows the proposition that ideas save, or that mere words save, even the words "Lord, Lord" (Mt 7:21). More solid witnesses to human dispositions lie in actions, which not only reveal relationships but make them real. In short, God and human existence are united by actions rather than words, and sometimes they accomplish this without or in spite of words.

Two other maxims should govern the way one moves from scriptural and theological ideas to a description of actual Christian life or spirituality. One pertains to the character of the experience that is involved. The language of spirituality readily appeals to experience in a unique way. But the consciousness of God as Spirit or the experience of God's grace in one's life has to be understood carefully. The topic of knowledge of the transcendent reality of God was discussed earlier. There can be no direct or unmediated knowledge of God; encounter is always particular, filtered through historical events, and experienced individually. But there are ways of making common sense out of the extensive witness to experiences of God and a community of God-consciousness. One maxim holds that people experience God but not directly as God. The negative dialectical principle holds that God transcends and thus exceeds all the predicates that experience generates. While God cannot be immediately experienced, one can realistically discern that some experiences, while they may be explained naturalistically, symbolically mediate God as Presence to consciousness in a mediating, self-negating but knowing way. The diffuse idea of God as Presence retains both the realism and the transcendence of the object of consciousness.

The other maxim applies to the normativity of the notions that describe spiritual life. The existential definition of spirituality, as the way persons lead their lives in relation to what is ultimate, means that there will be as many distinct and unique spiritualities as there are human beings. The individuality of situation and person always conditions the internalization of spiritual authority. Objective spirituality drawn from history and theology are always transformed by personal appropriation in a given context and situation.

With such cautions in mind, the traditions of scripture and theological tradition offer strong sets of ideas and values that can be applied to Christian life today.

God as Spirit within Human Freedom

Can the biblical and theological accounts of how God as Spirit works in the human subject find experiential correlates in actual human experience? Neither biblical story nor theological construct can be understood as descriptions of direct experiences of God or observations of actual psychological experiences. They are expressions of faith that correspond to the biblical interpretations of God's grace that the Bible, or Jesus's teachings, or Christian theological interpretations associate with God's intentions and will for human existence. Such testimonies of faith are not scarce in human history. It should be clear that, if grace abounds in human existence, if the presence of God as loving Spirit is universal with existence itself, its push toward welcoming the stranger and being kind to the neighbor are not limited to Jews and Christians. One might indeed expect that the core values of Christian spirituality are shared among the religions. The commandments set before Israel through Moses or the teachings of Jesus on the virtuous life are found elsewhere. The point is not to limit the work of God as Spirit in human freedom to a Christian anthropology and spirituality by particular intervention. It is rather to describe the structure of how God as Spirit opens up human freedom in response to transcendent values for human fulfillment everywhere. Although the tradition describes Christian spirituality, it has general humanistic relevance. If these experiences are found in other religions, that surely does not subtract from their value.

Augustine thinks of the fundamental Christian response to God as Spirit working within human beings as openness and responsiveness to value outside the self. He operates from a dour sense of pervasive sin and a self in bondage to self-concern. The Spirit offers divine help that breaks open this fundamentally closed disposition and expands the horizon of freedom to respond to every kind of value that solicits freedom out of itself. This structure is elementary. Where does reverence for creation itself and for the discrete kinds of being come from, and how is it grounded? Why do so many people radiate gratitude for life itself and everything positive in it? On Augustine's principles, wherever one finds these basic attitudes toward persons other than the self, to the values that promote social cohesion, there God as Spirit is at work. Augustine's relevance plainly appears in his positive experience of being summoned out of himself in response to something so much larger than himself and that filled his life with direction and purpose.

As noted earlier, Aquinas reads the fundamental effect of God as Spirit in the human spirit as the bundle of classic Christian virtues of faith, hope, and love of God. These so-called theological virtues could be multiplied and described at length because all virtue is carried by the power of God as Spirit. Virtues are foundational dispositions that generate and facilitate positive human actions or behaviors. Faith is conscious responsive commitment to God and God's will as mediated by Jesus; hope is absolute trust in a future that will ultimately rest in God's loving hands; love is the outwardly oriented attachment to God and all God's friends that directs day-to-day living. It bears repetition that these fundamental orientations are joined by a whole list of virtues that are both personal and social and supported by God as Spirit. They describe countless lives across all the ethnic, cultural, and religious boundaries that define the human race.

For Martin Luther, the Spirit of God alone accounts for human beings recognizing their impotence for self-salvation, especially relative to their moral failure, and for their turning to God for forgiveness. On the one hand, the hyperactivity of our age may neglect reflection on the self out of a feeling of entitlement; on the other hand, people may operate out of a low self-esteem that hides within activity. In either case the question remains: where is the self within the activity? Luther describes Christian faith as mediating a sense of divine acceptance and affirmation of the human person that transforms human lives. Luther's Christian spirituality of divine love and a response of gratitude account for a liberation that transfigures the whole life of a person and leads to selfless action. Luther's language of grace focuses on Christ, but God as Spirit is the internal power that moves a person to faith.

In many ways Calvin internalizes Luther's theology of grace and explicitly turns it toward action. Personal justification is not static but forms a relationship that is continually acted out in the responsibilities of life: in family, in one's work, in larger social and political relationships. One's unity with God and with other people are lived relationships that Calvin saw as potentially becoming stronger in the practice. Calvin wrote a short manual of the Christian life into his systematic theology, but more important than the ascetic details is the basic observation that faithfully living life in Geneva, including family, work, and social responsibilities, strengthens personal union with God.

Rahner, who accepts the universalism of the work of God as Spirit, describes how the work of the Spirit, grace, manifests itself in ways that can be witnessed outside the Christian sphere. Ask the question and it answers itself: other than the explicit mediation of God through Jesus of Nazareth, what virtue found in Christianity cannot be found outside it? One can find a sense of moral failure and the experience of transformation, faith in ultimate reality, confidence in the face of death, hope in an absolute future, and altruistic love in other religious traditions and in ordinary moral life. Rahner's transcendental thinking allows him to discover implicit faith in God, latent love of God, and the equivalent of hope in an absolute future within the everyday commitments of secular existence. By Augustine's standards, these are the workings of grace. Fundamental faith in human existence itself as an absolute value implies a basis for it in ultimacy. Courage in the face of challenge and especially death implies a ground for basic trust or hope. Deep respect for other human beings entails a foundation that authenticates their value. In sum, a Christian theology of the working of God as Spirit shows that grace is more operative in the world than is generally recognized.

Personal Spirituality in the Public Sphere

Spirituality includes the way groups lead their lives guided by a relation to ultimate reality. Personal life normally cannot be cleanly restricted to a private or individual sphere; when behavior becomes corporate, it is usually public, and it assumes some social relevance. The obvious examples of this are the public faith traditions that are maintained by various institutional structures. Scripture is full of references to God as Spirit not simply being present and active to individuals, but also to Israel corporately. The Jesus movement that followed Jesus became the Christian church. Churches and synagogues exist in a symbiotic relationship with the individuals that are their members; spirituality refers to both the communitarian life of the faith tradition, including its institutional forms, and the individual lives of members.

The institutionalization of a faith tradition, in its public corporate life, has a primary function of maintaining a tradition across time. Its structures guarantee the ministry that nurtures the community's spirituality in successive generations. A complete account of spirituality would include the many practices of particular traditions in their actual forms of religious or spiritual exercises. But institutionalized practices have another function of being the face of a spiritual tradition, its representation to the surrounding social world. When a faith tradition thinks of its revelation not as a private communication for a select group but for humankind generally, the public face of a group spirituality will represent it to the world and invite participation. It will also seek to exert a positive influence on society. If love of God includes love of neighbor on a personal level, it would be hard to imagine a communal Christian spirituality that did not exercise a public compassion for human suffering and a desire to ameliorate tragic situations of social suffering.

Ernst Troeltsch, after analyzing the history of the church in terms of its social relationship with society, formulated two main types of how the corporate spirituality of the church relates to society at large. He gave the name "church type" to churches that become public institutions that fit into society in a way that is not disruptive of society but representative of a way of life that is integrated and nurturing of the common good. He gave the name "sect type" to churches that distinguish themselves from the ordinary social and political sphere either by a stricter moral code, or nonparticipation in practices of law enforcement or war, and sometimes withdrawal from town or city life.[5] The emergence of monasticism in early Christianity illustrates some of the traits of separatist Christian life. The stress in sectarian spirituality lies in a relationship with God and a more attenuated relationship to society as a whole by an external representative witness. The example of monasticism, however, teaches a larger lesson. Monasticism was contained within a larger institutional tradition. Christian spirituality cannot really be tightly contained or restrained by institutional structures and will always push them to change to meet the historical present. The World Council of Churches demonstrates that Christian spirituality can take many different forms on a public level.

A good example of this can be found in the logic of liberation theologies that was discussed in Chapter 4. A liberation theology has an accompanying liberation spirituality that understands Christian revelation, faith, and ethics as promoting human flourishing in this life; it reacts against social, political, and cultural structures that attack human life and cause human suffering; it promotes a

---

[5] Ernst Troeltsch, "Sect-type and Church-type Contrasted," in *The Social Teaching of the Christian Churches* (New York: Harper Torchbooks, 1960), 331–43.

spirituality of engagement in society. Whole congregations can assume a liberationist character; liberation spirituality often animates a
segment of a larger church; it stimulates subgroups whose corporate
spirituality accents social and political involvement. But this is easier
in a religiously homogeneous situation. In a situation of religious
pluralism, the effectiveness of a liberationist spirituality, however
strongly it may be motivated by a specific religious spiritual tradition, may be more successful with a humanist branding than with
a denominational identity.

Resistance, Creativity, and Hope

This final section relates Christian theology and spirituality to
the cosmic pessimism of our time. The key to a credible response
to pessimism lies in keeping Christian theology and spirituality
together. Theology aims at understanding; spirituality consists of
action. The one is critical thinking; the other is reflective behavior.
They are distinct but mutually informative, and each needs the
other in order to be itself. Theology derives from spirituality, as a
reflective expression of the rationale of spiritual life. Spirituality
provides the verification of theology. Theology contains existential
truth that can only be verified in practice. Together they provide
the elements that constitute the meaningfulness of Christian faith.
Therefore, the doctrines of God as creator, the revealing mediation
and representation of Jesus Christ, and the doctrine of God as Spirit
contain the elements of a spirituality of action that can overcome
pessimism and communicate a meaningful humanism when they
are put into practice.

An essential feature of a response to cosmic pessimism lies in
the theology of resurrection to eternal life together with the spirituality implicit in the belief. Many problems surround the belief in
eternal life in today's metaphysically skeptical and scientifically
critical culture. It was easier in a prescientific and enchanted age
of spirits and demons to accept another world that transcended
the earthly sphere but kept impinging upon it. In the disenchanted
world of science the spiritual has to become wedded to the physical

in a non-duality without exception. The spiritual can no longer be separated from the material but has to be found within it. We cannot conceive mind without brain or spirit without physical organism. Resurrection cannot mean, or at least we can no longer imagine, the soul in the machine, with an autonomous existence, escaping into a world of spirit no longer associated with time and space.

But on the same premises, neither can God be imagined. For God to be God requires a transcendence that excludes limiting God to the dimensions of finitude. One affirms the reality of the creating source of being and the wholly encompassing and constantly sustaining power of being that is God by denying God's finitude. Since that dialectical conception of God, arrived at by contrast and negation, transcends space and time, one affirms God as creator who contains all reality within itself at all times. One can affirm God as *totum simul*, but one cannot escape finitude to comprehend it, except by negation.[6] Nevertheless, by holding on to God as the fullness of being, one paradoxically grounds one's own autonomy and identity as dependent on it and subsistent in its power. Clinging to God affirms one's own being as a unique individual.

The unimaginable creator God also offers a certain mysterious intelligibility to the idea of resurrection. What God has created and will create from the human perspective never escapes from God's presence to God's self. God holds all things within the power of God's being, acting, grounding, creating, mystery, and presence. Human beings, from their tiny momentary perspective of past, present, and future in time, can speak of God's memory of our past. But if God is God, then all things remain eternally present, *simul,* within the Godhead. What appears to human consciousness as resurrection has that status only by reason of the limited perspective of time and space. In short, existence within the sphere of God or, in our reckoning, God's memory, utterly transcends physicality in the same measure that it includes it within divine Presence. A physicalist imagination

---

[6] *Totum simul* is translated literally as "all at once"; it provides a shorthand definition of eternity. All reality, including all space and time, is compressed into the reality of God's immediate present and self-presence, as an eternity that has no beginning or end and contains within itself the fullness of reality. Here the phrase serves as a symbol of absolute incomprehensible mystery.

or an anthropomorphic conception of resurrection renders it in some childish imaginable form. In the same measure the transcendent incomprehensible mystery of creation itself renders resurrection into a somewhat logical entailment of a personal creator God. Resurrection occurs in an utterly transcendent sphere. It is concomitant within creation as the creating memory of God.

It was noted in Chapter 3 that Islamic faith underlines the fact that God keeps an account of time and all that happens in it. The non-forgetful creating of God ensures the meaningfulness of human existence. The God of mercy remembers the constructive actions that enhance life; God preserves, in creating memory, the productive work and its benefits.

The idea of God as eternal creator means that what God creates continues to exist within the reality of God as time continuously runs out on worldly beings. The fleeting existence of things in time is contained all at once in the infinite and eternal one. For it to be otherwise would implicitly deny the transcendent character of God. The limits of the human imagination continually pull God into the limits of space and time and distort God's transcendence. Concepts like the self-limitation of God, or the idea that God is in process, or that God suffers, for all their emotional effectiveness, fundamentally fail to recognize the complete otherness of God from the finite created reality that God sustains in existence. God not only keeps alive whatever lives in the temporal moment, but all of created reality continues to subsist in the creating memory of God. God's memory totally transcends a human memory that only holds the past for a time in pale image; God's memory, being God's and being creative, sustains finite reality in God's self-present actuality.

God continually creates finite reality that is other than God's self and holds it in time. God as Spirit points to the dynamism of God creating. But God also co-creates along with the dynamism and agency of what God is creating. All finite reality is in motion with some kind of immanent energy that science in various ways tries to render intelligible with its algorithms. Finitude is intrinsically in process, always generating new being. Human beings have the ability to participate in this perpetual motion intentionally with a reflective consciousness. This conscious intentionality raises the processes of finitude to a distinctly new level where some measure of freedom can orient creation to planned effect. In sharp, clear terms, human freedom has the power to co-create eternal meaning. Measured on the scale of human flourishing and care for earth's integrity, this eternal meaning will share positive and negative value; creating meaning involves the sphere of morality. The doctrine of creation, therefore, entails that there can be no lack of meaning in the sphere of human existence; it is there within the very exercise of freedom. Human freedom is always creating some meaning that is eternal within God's memory. Spirituality contains the invitation, in so many different ways, to construct meaning that is positive.

In Chapter 4, the discussion turned to liberation theology in response to cosmic pessimism. Based on foundational ethical imperatives that arise out of negative contrast experiences, the discussion showed how religious or spiritual consciousness harbors a moral impulse to right the wrong and create new positive structures that replace dehumanizing forces. The line of thinking in that proposal moves from thinking in terms of personal experiences toward actions that lead toward building social patterns of existence that are liberating. But one can also think in the opposite direction. Positive social structures that involve corporate existence structured by positive relationships generate in their turn habits of thinking and acting that govern individual lives. This describes, for example, the fundamental logic of family nurture of early human life. Liberation theologies that describe building just structuring of human life in all aspects of society, therefore, also describe the character of the meaning that Christianity holds out to personal spirituality. It reflects exactly the categorical imperative found in the pattern of Jesus's ministry and teaching; that is, so act that all that you do fosters the rule of God. Think of personal life as a participation in the intentionality of the creator, a dynamic intentionality for human existence that helps build structures into human living that will enhance the human character of life: mutual respect among individuals, behavior patterns that reflect a reverence for being itself, and a basic moral disposition that guides one in that direction.

✳

This introduction to Christian theology recognizes the distinctive historical situation provided by developed Western culture. At no time has human existence become so immersed in technological development. Most people of a certain age have a sense of how deeply the devices that help us live more fully also influence the desires, values, and goals we actually live by. As essential tasks get simpler and life gets faster and the tools of life become more complex, life seems to be fully spent on the surface. Knowledge of facts grow and understanding becomes more superficial; people see more and think less. Answers to the perennial questions about the nature of the good life are constantly shifting beneath our feet. It is difficult for theology to keep up with culture, and when it does, one always has to worry about the price paid for relevancy.

It is hard to measure how deeply metaphysical skepticism, relativism, and cosmic pessimism affect developed Western culture. One senses it might be misguided to try to quantify the permutations of these cultural drifts. But it would be a more serious mistake to ignore the pragmatic challenges to a metaphysical imagination, the power of relativism to trivialize a search for the constant and the universal, for the things that bind human beings together rather than distinguish and separate them. One of the deepest challenges to religious consciousness has to be its seeming irrelevance; only exceptionally does it make much difference in the public sphere; it appeals mainly to personal need and self-help. And then pessimism fuels apathy. If these terms reflect forces at work in contemporary intellectual and more widespread reflective culture, one cannot ignore them or pretend that they are not there.

In response to the West's new secular scientific culture, this introduction to Christian theology makes three basic moves. First, it turns to religious experience, which is in ample supply in the world. It uses a simple theory of religious consciousness, which Christian theology calls revelation, that contains three elements: (a) an awareness of transcendent reality, (b) that is mediated through some historical object or event, and (c) that requires a resonance within human subjectivity that attends to, recognizes, receives, and interprets the revelatory communication.

Second, this three-dimensional analysis of the elements of religious consciousness, secondly, correlates fairly closely with the three core doctrines of Christian teaching. They teach about the creator God, how God is mediated to Christian consciousness through Jesus of Nazareth, and they maintain a strong doctrine of the immanence of the creator God who, as Spirit, is present to and stimulates religious response from inside human consciousness.

Third, these three doctrines are loosely coordinated with the three issues that theology has to address in our time: skepticism, relativism, and pessimism. This correlation may be somewhat forced, but it is convenient. A theology of God has to deal with metaphysical skepticism; Jesus Christ has to be defended against relativism and can be by acknowledging the positive and necessary character of religious pluralism. Christianity has no place for pessimism; it uses historical realism to react against a seemingly cosmic negativity and shows how meaning and meaning-making is intrinsic to human existence accompanied by God. It is astonishing how many basic category mistakes underlie these deeply influential cultural drifts. God is not threatened by human science, historical diversity, or evil; God provides the possibility for their ultimate meaningfulness.

Finally, the conclusion of this representation of the discipline of theology as a positive academic discipline can be formulated precisely in response to cosmic pessimism. Christianity provides meaning for human life by stimulating resistance to evil in the world and offering grounds for creativity and for hope. God is the ground of creativity and meaning; and human existence is creation conscious of itself and the conscious subject of hope.

Index

Printed in the USA
CPSIA information can be obtained
at www.ICGtesting.com
LVHW011758040824
787333LV00003B/298

9 781626 984882